tempt

tempt

Decadent and delicious
chocolate recipes

This edition published by Parragon Books Ltd in 2015
LOVE FOOD is an imprint of Parragon Books Ltd

Parragon Books Ltd
Chartist House
15–17 Trim Street
Bath BA1 1HA, UK
www.parragon.com/lovefood

ISBN 978-1-4723-9254-1

Printed in China

New recipes by Mima Sinclair
New photography by Mike Cooper
New home economy by Lincoln Jefferson
Introduction and incidental text by Christine McFadden
Designed by Bethan Kalynka

Notes for the Reader
This book uses both metric and imperial measurements. Follow the same units of
measurement throughout; do not mix metric and imperial. All spoon measurements are
level: teaspoons are assumed to be 5 ml, and tablespoons are assumed to be 15 ml. Unless
otherwise stated, milk is assumed to be full fat, eggs and individual vegetables are medium,
pepper is freshly ground black pepper and salt is table salt. Unless otherwise stated, all root
vegetables should be peeled prior to using.

The times given are an approximate guide only. Preparation times differ according to the
techniques used by different people and the cooking times may also vary from those given.

Contents

FOOD OF THE GODS

Most of us probably don't realize that chocolate, probably the most loved and addictive confectionery of all, comes from the fruit of the cacao tree, or *Theobroma cacao*, from the Greek, meaning 'food of the gods'.

Most of us also think of chocolate as a solid confectionery, although for much of its long history it was enjoyed as a drink rather than as something to be eaten.

So how and when did this transformation from bean to beverage to bar take place?

From bean to beverage

In the early 1500s, the explorer Christopher Columbus discovered cacao beans in Central America while searching for a route to the spice islands in the East. The native Aztecs thought the beans had magical powers, and even used them as a kind of primitive currency. The story goes that they bartered a sack of their precious beans for some of Columbus's merchandise. They also offered him their special drink made from crushed beans laced with chillies and cornmeal. Unaware of the their future economic worth, Columbus took some beans to Spain, more out of curiosity than because he enjoyed the rather unpalatable drink.

Moving on about twenty years, the Spanish conquistador Hernando Cortés arrived on the scene. Unlike Columbus, he quickly caught on to the bean's enormous potential, and he, too, took beans back to Spain, along with a recipe for xocolatl, the Aztecs' chocolate drink. Just as he predicted, the drink became very fashionable among the wealthy cognoscenti. Meanwhile, the Spanish conquistadors made their fortunes by establishing cacao plantations in Central America and elsewhere. For them, money really did grow on trees.

Chocolate travels the world

In 1580, Spain became home to the first ever chocolate-processing plant. From then on there was no holding it back. The passion for chocolate drinking spread like wildfire through Europe, and eventually to America and the rest of the world.

Sugar and spice

By the late 16th century, chocolate manufacturing had become more sophisticated, and the drink was certainly more palatable. Sugar, a novel ingredient at the time, and fragrant spices – cinnamon, vanilla and musk, for example – were added to the roasted ground beans. The mix was ground again to a fine paste, which, in turn, was moulded into chunky blocks. The blocks were used for making a drink, just as they are in Spain and Mexico today.

From beverage to bar

As the early chocolate-makers discovered, cacao contains cacao butter, which produced unappetising fatty globules on the surface of the drink. Eventually a Dutch chemist figured out a way of separating the cacao butter and he invented a hydraulic press that successfully dealt with the problem.

But now there was a new problem: what to do with all that valuable cacao butter? Yet again a solution was found: the melted cacao butter was mixed with ground cacao beans and sugar to make a smooth paste that was liquid enough to pour into a mould. It was from this novel idea that 'eating chocolate' was developed.

Growing, Harvesting
and Processing

The cacao tree grows only in tropical regions 10 degrees either side of the Equator. The Ivory Coast, Ghana and Indonesia are the world's largest producers, followed by Cameroon, Nigeria, Brazil, Ecuador, the Dominican Republic, Malaysia and Togo.

The pointed fruit or pods sprout directly from the tree's trunk and branches. About 20 cm/8 inches long, they come in gloriously flamboyant colours – bright green, red, purple, yellow and gold – the hue changing as they ripen. Inside the pod are the precious beans, nestling in a cocoon of sweetish white pulp.

Bean varieties and flavours

There are three main types of bean:

Criollo: Now almost extinct, this is the finest, most expensive, most sort-after cacao. It has an exceptional flavour and aroma.

Forastero: Making up most of the world's production, this is a hardy variety with robust flavours. More bitter than Criollo, it's used mainly for blending with other beans.

Trinitario: Bred in Trinidad in the 18th century, this is a hybrid of Criollo and Forasterio. The flavour combines the robustness of Forasterio and the delicacy of Criollo.

Processing

The transformation from plump pods to deluxe chocolate is one that draws equally on the skills of both the grower and the chocolate-maker.

The process begins when the ripe pods are harvested. They are cut from the trees, then left to rest for a week to ten days before the husks are split in two and the beans and surrounding pulp are scooped out.

Next comes the all-important fermentation – this is crucial for developing the final flavour and aroma of the chocolate. The beans and pulp are piled in a wooden box or on banana leaves, covered and left for six to seven days while micro-organisms do their work. As the beans ferment they darken, and the wonderful aroma of cocoa begins to emerge.

The beans are dried in the sun for up to two weeks. They are then ready to be shovelled into sacks and shipped across the world to the chocolate manufacturers, where the transformation continues.

Roasting

When they arrive at the factory, the beans are cleaned, graded and then roasted. A crucial part of the process, roasting develops the flavour and enriches the colour of the bean. It's vital to get it right, otherwise the flavour will be ruined.

Grinding

The roasted beans are passed through a winnowing machine that blows off the outer shell. The nibs – the edible heart of the bean – are then ground between metal rollers, producing a liquid paste called cocoa mass or liquor. This consists of about 45 per cent cocoa solids and 55 per cent cocoa butter – a unique fat that is solid at room temperature but miraculously melts in the mouth.

Conching

To create the velvety smooth chocolate we love, the liquid chocolate is gently heated and stirred in a conching machine. This, in turn, fine tunes the texture and flavour. Cheap chocolate is conched for as little as 12 hours, while top-quality chocolate is conched for up to a week.

Tempering

The final step in the process, tempering involves heating and cooling the chocolate to very precise temperatures. This produces top-notch chocolate with a gorgeous sheen, great texture and a cracking good snap.

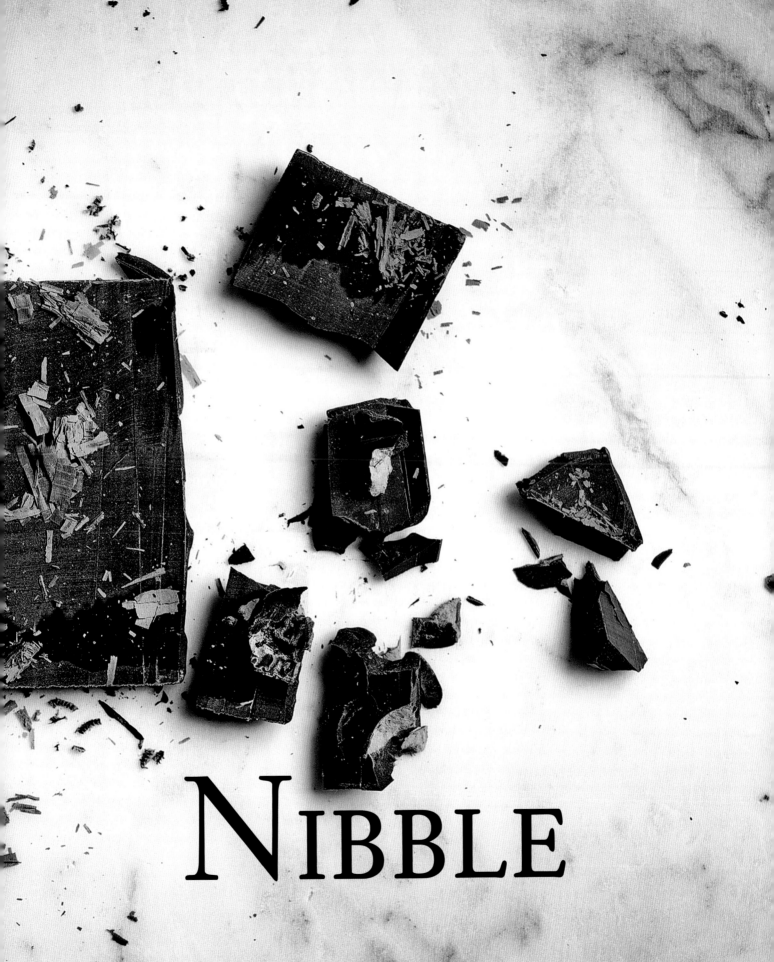

NIBBLE

CHOCOLATE PRETZEL
Fudge Squares

These are so easy to make. The salty pretzels counteract the rich sweetness of the chocolate and condensed milk.

Makes 16

Prep: 15 mins   Cook: 8–10 mins, plus setting

Ingredients

175 g/6 oz mini pretzels

1 tbsp sunflower oil, for oiling

2 tbsp unsalted butter, diced

300 g/10½ oz milk chocolate chips

400 g/14 oz canned sweetened full-fat condensed milk

1 tsp vanilla extract

1. Roughly chop 55 g/2 oz of the pretzels.

2. Lightly brush a 25-cm/10-inch square baking tin with the oil and line it with non-stick baking paper, snipping diagonally into the corners, then pressing the paper into the tin so that the base and sides are lined. There should be a 5-cm/2-inch overhang on all sides.

3. Put the butter, chocolate chips, condensed milk and vanilla extract into a heatproof bowl set over a saucepan of gently simmering water and heat, stirring occasionally, for 8–10 minutes, or until the chocolate has just melted and the mixture is smooth and warm but not hot. Remove from the heat and stir in the chopped pretzels.

4. Pour the mixture into the prepared tin, smooth the surface with a spatula and push in the whole pretzels. Leave to cool for 1 hour. Cover with clingfilm, then chill in the refrigerator for 1–2 hours, or until firm.

5. Lift the fudge out of the tin, peel off the paper and cut it into 16 squares. Store in an airtight container in a cool, dry place for up to 2 weeks.

WHITE CHOCOLATE
Rocky Road

Makes 20

When cooking with white chocolate use a brand that contains cocoa butter. White chocolate has a delicate structure and the cocoa butter helps it withstand heating.

Prep: 30 mins, plus chilling   Cook: 10 mins

Ingredients

200 g/7 oz white chocolate

70 g/2½ oz butter

100 g/3½ oz shortbread biscuits

15 g/½ oz mini pink and white marshmallows

100 g/3½ oz glacé cherries, halved

1 tbsp freeze-dried raspberries

1. Line a 20-cm/8-inch square cake tin with baking paper.

2. Break the chocolate into small pieces and cut the butter into cubes. Place both in a heatproof bowl set over a saucepan of gently simmering water and heat until melted.

3. Place the biscuits in a polythene bag, seal the bag and gently crush the biscuits with a rolling pin to make small pieces. Add them to the melted chocolate mixture, then stir in the marshmallows and two thirds of the cherries.

4. Spoon the mixture into the tin, spreading evenly. Place the remaining cherries on the surface and scatter over the raspberries.

5. Leave to set in a cool place for about 1 hour.

6. Cut into 20 squares and serve.

NUTTY CHOCOLATE
Puddles

Makes 24–30

Chocolate puddles are adult chocolate buttons and you won't meet anyone who wouldn't gladly receive a little box of these!

Prep: 20 mins, plus cooling and setting   Cook: 10 mins

Ingredients

10 g/¼ oz each pistachio nuts, almonds, hazelnuts and macadamia nuts

100 g/3½ oz plain chocolate, finely chopped

100 g/3½ oz milk chocolate, finely chopped

100 g/3½ oz white chocolate, finely chopped

1. Preheat the oven to 200°C/400°F/Gas Mark 6. Spread the nuts over a large baking tray and roast in the preheated oven for 5–6 minutes until golden. Roughly chop into small pieces and leave to cool.

2. Put the plain chocolate, milk chocolate and white chocolate into separate heatproof bowls set over saucepans of gently simmering water and heat until melted. Remove from the heat and leave to cool for 1–2 minutes.

3. Spoon generous teaspoons of the chocolate onto greaseproof paper to make 8–10 puddles of each type of chocolate. Scatter over the chopped nuts and leave to cool and set firm.

4. Carefully remove the set puddles from the paper. Store in an airtight container in a cool place, but not in the refrigerator, for up to 2 weeks.

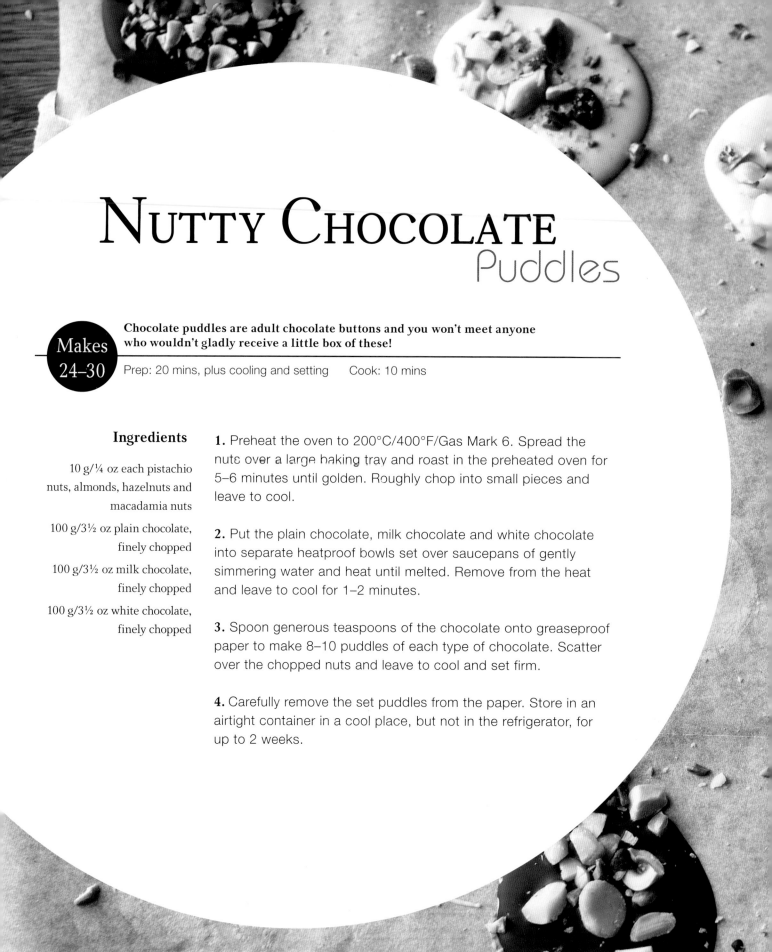

VARIATION
Try adding finely chopped dried fruit, such as sour cherries or crystallized ginger, to the nut mix; or you could swirl the different chocolates together in one puddle.

Salted Caramel &
Chocolate Bites

Makes 20

Sea salt and caramel is one of the classic combinations, enhanced here by the addition of crunchy walnuts.

Prep: 30 mins   Cook: 35–40 mins

Ingredients

1 tbsp sunflower oil, for oiling

200 g/7 oz plain chocolate, roughly chopped

150 g/5½ oz unsalted butter

2 eggs

175 g/6 oz soft light brown sugar

55 g/2 oz plain flour

1 tsp baking powder

55 g/2 oz walnut pieces, roughly chopped

6 tbsp dulce de leche (caramel sauce)

1 tbsp sea salt

1. Preheat the oven to 160°C/325°F/Gas Mark 3. Lightly brush a 20-cm/8-inch square baking tin with oil. Line it with non-stick baking paper, snipping diagonally into the corners, then pressing the paper into the tin so that the base and sides are lined.

2. Put 70 g/2½ oz of the chocolate and all the butter into a heatproof bowl, set the bowl over a saucepan of gently simmering water and heat, stirring occasionally, until melted.

3. Put the eggs and sugar into a mixing bowl, then sift in the flour and baking powder. Stir in the melted chocolate mixture and beat together until blended. Add the walnuts and remaining chocolate and stir together. Pour the mixture into the prepared tin and smooth the surface using a spatula.

4. Put the dulce de leche into a small mixing bowl and beat, then swirl it through the chocolate mixture using a fork. Scatter over the sea salt and bake in the preheated oven for 30–35 minutes, or until the cake begins to shrink slightly from the sides of the tin. Leave to cool in the tin for 1 hour.

5. Lift the cake out of the tin, peel off the paper and cut it into 20 squares. Store in an airtight container in a cool, dry place for up to 2 days.

CHOCOLATE ORANGE
Cannoli

Makes 20–24

One of chocolate's most natural pairing ingredients is orange. In this recipe the oil in the grated orange rind brings out the bittersweet flavour of the plain chocolate.

Prep: 40 mins, plus chilling   Cook: 25 mins

Ingredients

1 egg

2 tbsp Marsala

175 g/6 oz Italian 00 flour

2 tsp caster sugar

pinch of salt

10 g/¼ oz flour, for dusting

1 tbsp sunflower oil, for brushing

sunflower oil, for deep-frying

10 g/¼ oz icing sugar, to decorate

Chocolate & Orange Filling

750 g/1 lb 10 oz ricotta cheese

2 tbsp brandy

2 tsp vanilla extract

2 tbsp cocoa powder

3 tbsp icing sugar

4 tbsp chopped glacé oranges

3 tbsp chopped plain chocolate

finely grated rind of 2 large oranges

pinch of ground cinnamon

1. Beat the egg and Marsala together. Put the flour, sugar and salt into a food processor and blend. With the motor running, slowly pour in the egg mixture until the ingredients just come together to form a dough. Turn out the dough onto a lightly floured work surface and knead. Roll into a ball, wrap in clingfilm and chill in the refrigerator for at least 1 hour.

2. Meanwhile, to make the filling, heat together the cheese, brandy and vanilla extract until creamy. Sift in the cocoa powder and icing sugar and stir in the glacé oranges, chocolate, orange rind and cinnamon. Cover and chill until required.

3. Cut the dough into four equal pieces. Use a pasta machine to roll one piece into a strip about 50 cm/20 inches long, or roll out on a lightly floured work surface until the dough is thin enough to see through. Cut out 4-cm/1½-inch squares. Brush some cannoli tubes with oil and diagonally roll a piece of dough around each. Use a dab of water to seal the corners where they meet and press firmly.

4. Heat enough oil for deep-frying to 180–190°C/ 350–375°F, or until a cube of bread browns in 30 seconds. Add 2–3 cannoli tubes at a time to the oil and fry until the pastry is golden brown and crisp. Use a slotted spoon to remove the tubes and transfer them to kitchen paper to drain. Continue until all the dough has been used, gently sliding the shells off the tubes, and re-oiling before using again.

5. Store in an airtight container for up to 3 days until required. Just before serving, use a piping bag or a spoon to fill the tubes from both ends. If you fill the cannoli in advance they will become soggy. Dust with icing sugar and serve immediately.

ESPRESSO Truffles

Makes 12

For a different twist on these luscious coffee truffles, simply replace the coffee with Irish cream liqueur or any orange-flavoured liqueur such as triple sec.

Prep: 40 mins   Cook: 5–10 mins, plus chilling

Ingredients

300 g/10½ oz plain chocolate, roughly chopped

2 tbsp double cream

1 tbsp strong espresso coffee, cooled

2 tbsp coffee liqueur

55 g/2 oz unsalted butter, softened and diced

edible gold leaf, to decorate (optional)

1. Put 100 g/3½ oz of the chocolate and all the cream in a heatproof bowl set over a saucepan of gently simmering water and heat until the chocolate is melted.

2. Remove from the heat, add the coffee, coffee liqueur and butter and whisk for 3–4 minutes, or until thickened. Transfer to an airtight container and chill in the refrigerator for 6–8 hours, or until firm.

3. Line a baking tray with non-stick baking paper. Scoop teaspoonfuls of the mixture and, using the palms of your hands, roll them into truffle-sized balls. Place the balls on the prepared tray, cover with clingfilm and freeze for 6–8 hours.

4. Put the remaining chocolate in a heatproof bowl, set the bowl over a saucepan of gently simmering water and heat until melted. Using two forks, dip each truffle into the chocolate to coat evenly. Return them to the prepared baking tray and chill in the refrigerator for 1–2 hours, or until firm.

5. Decorate each truffle with edible gold leaf, if using. Store in an airtight container in the refrigerator for up to 5 days.

CHOCOLATE COOKIE
Dough Kisses

Makes 20

Cookie dough is a classic flavour and is made even more moreish with these little home-made chocolate kisses!

Prep: 25 mins, plus chilling   Cook: 12 mins, plus cooling

Ingredients

125 g/4½ oz butter, softened

75 g/2¾ oz soft light brown sugar

75 g/2¾ oz granulated sugar

½ tsp vanilla extract

1 egg

250 g/9 oz plain flour

½ tsp bicarbonate of soda

100 g/3½ oz chocolate chips

200 g/7 oz plain chocolate

50 ml/2 fl oz double cream

1. Preheat the oven to 180°C/350°F/Gas Mark 4. Line three baking sheets with greaseproof paper or silicone sheets. Whisk together the butter, brown sugar and granulated sugar until just combined. Add the vanilla extract and egg and beat until combined.

2. Sift together the flour and bicarbonate of soda into a separate bowl, then gradually add to the butter mixture until just combined. Fold through the chocolate chips and bring the dough together with your hands. Wrap in clingfilm and chill in the refrigerator for 30 minutes.

3. Put the chocolate and cream into a heatproof bowl set over a saucepan of gently simmering water and heat until the chocolate is melted. Leave to cool for 15 minutes until it is just beginning to thicken.

4. Spoon the chocolate into a piping bag fitted with a 1-cm/½-inch round nozzle and set aside for 15 minutes, or until thick enough to pipe out chocolate drops. Pipe twenty 2 x 2-cm/¾ x ¾-inch mounds onto one of the prepared baking sheets. Chill in the refrigerator until hard.

5. Make 20 even-sized balls of cookie dough and place on the remaining prepared baking sheets, spaced well apart to allow for spreading. Bake in the preheated oven for 10 minutes until just golden and slightly undercooked.

6. Leave the cookies to cool on the sheets for 15 minutes, then press a chocolate kiss into the centre of each. Leave on the sheets to cool completely.

VARIATION
Want to eat the cookie dough raw? Leave out the egg and add 1–2 tablespoons of milk. Chill the dough and eat it unbaked.

MILK & COOKIE
Shots

Refreshing almond milk served in a chocolate-lined, wholegrain hazelnut cookie – who said eating healthily was dull?

Prep: 35 mins, plus chilling   Cook: 18–20 mins

Ingredients

1 tbsp coconut oil, for oiling

6 tbsp coconut oil, at room temperature

55 g/2 oz light muscovado sugar

½ tsp natural vanilla extract

25 g/1 oz ground hazelnuts

25 g/1 oz ground golden linseeds

115 g/4 oz plain wholemeal flour

1 egg yolk

100 g/3½ oz plain chocolate, 70% cocoa solids

150 ml/5 fl oz unsweetened almond milk

1. Lightly oil six 90-ml/3-fl oz dariole moulds and line each base with a round of non-stick baking paper.

2. Beat together the coconut oil, sugar and vanilla extract in a mixing bowl or food processor until light and creamy. Add the hazelnuts and linseeds, then add the flour and egg yolk, and beat together. Finely chop 30 g/1 oz of the chocolate and mix into the cookie crumbs. Using your hands, squeeze the dough into crumbly clumps.

3. Divide the mixture between the prepared moulds, then level with the back of a teaspoon. Transfer to a baking tray and chill in the refrigerator for 20 minutes. Meanwhile, preheat the oven to 180°C/350°F/Gas Mark 4.

4. Bake in the preheated oven for 13–15 minutes, until golden brown, then reshape the inside of the cups with the back of a small teaspoon. Leave to cool for 30 minutes.

5. Loosen the edges of the cups with a small, round bladed knife and remove from the tin. Return to the tray and chill in the refrigerator for at least 1 hour until firmly set.

6. Break the remaining chocolate into a bowl set over a saucepan of gently simmering water and heat until melted. Add spoonfuls of melted chocolate to the cookie cups, tilting to cover the insides evenly with chocolate. Chill for at least 30 minutes. When ready to serve, pour in the almond milk and serve on small saucers.

NIBBLE

When choosing chocolate, it's useful to know what to look for in terms of quality. Confusingly, chocolate classification and labelling requirements vary between countries. The important factor is the ingredients list on the wrapper. Beware if sugar appears near the top of the list – it means that it makes up a large proportion of the chocolate and the quality will be inferior.

Eating chocolate

There are three basic types:

Plain: This is made from cocoa solids sweetened with sugar and blended with extra cocoa butter. The higher the proportion of cocoa solids, the better the chocolate. Fifty per cent is the preferred minimum, while for chocoholics 70–80 per cent is even more desirable. Top-quality dark chocolate contains a proportionately small amount of sugar. Though intended primarily for eating, it can also be used for cooking.

Milk: This contains milk solids, cocoa butter and sugar. A good brand will have about 40 per cent cocoa solids, but most mass-produced milk chocolate contains only 20 per cent with a correspondingly high amount of sugar, sometimes up to 60 per cent, to make up the bulk.

White: This is a mixture of cocoa butter, milk solids and up to 60 per cent sugar. It usually contains no cocoa solids and as such, lacks depth of flavour, and can seize when heated. Sometimes synthetic vanilla is added to give it a boost.

How to recognize quality

When we try to assess chocolate quality, all our senses – sight, smell, sound, touch and taste – come into play:

Appearance: Dark chocolate should be smooth, brilliantly shiny and dark mahogany in colour.

Smell: Chocolate should smell of chocolate, and not excessively sweet.

Sound: Chocolate should be crisp and make a distinct 'snap' when broken.

Touch: Chocolate with a high cocoa butter content should start to melt when you hold it. In the mouth it should feel ultra-smooth and melt instantly.

Taste: Quality chocolate contains complex flavours and aromas. There should be bitterness with a hint of acidity, sweetness tempered by a hint of sourness, and just a touch of saltiness to help release the aromas.

Storing chocolate

Humidity and heat are chocolate's greatest enemies; both can cause a 'bloom' to appear on the surface. The ideal temperature is 10–15°C/50–59°F – slightly warmer than the refrigerator – and the humidity level should be about 50 per cent. Chocolate absorbs surrounding odours easily, even when wrapped, so store it in an airtight container.

PLAIN CHOCOLATE &
Peanut Butter Energy Balls

Makes 8

These energising healthy morsels, full of crunchy nuts, creamy peanut butter and rich dark chocolate, have no added sugar.

Prep: 15 mins, plus chilling   Cook: None

Ingredients

50 g/1¾ oz ground almonds

60 g/2¼ oz unsweetened peanut butter

20 g/¾ oz unsalted peanuts, roughly chopped

3 tbsp linseeds

30 g/1 oz plain chocolate, 85% cocoa solids, finely chopped

pinch of sea salt

1 tsp cocoa powder

1. Put the ground almonds in a food processor and process for 1 minute until you have the texture of rough flour.

2. Put the peanut butter, peanuts, linseeds, chocolate and salt into a bowl and mix. Add the almond flour, reserving 1½ tablespoons. Mix until you have a texture resembling chunky clay.

3. Sprinkle the reserved almond flour and the cocoa powder onto a plate and mix with a teaspoon. Shape a tablespoon of the peanut mixture into a ball using your palms. Roll it in the cocoa powder mixture, then transfer to a plate. Make a further seven balls in the same way.

4. Cover and chill in the refrigerator for at least 30 minutes, or up to 2 days.

VARIATION
If the coating of cocoa powder is too bitter and strong for your taste, substitute it with a teaspoon of ground cinnamon.

INDULGENT WHISKY
Fudge

If you are a chocolate and whisky lover, this is the perfect edible treat for you. You can use a good brandy instead of whisky, if you prefer.

Prep: 15 mins   Cook: 10–15 mins, plus setting

Ingredients

1 tbsp sunflower oil, for oiling

250 g/9 oz soft light brown sugar

100 g/3½ oz unsalted butter, diced

400 g/14 oz canned sweetened full-fat condensed milk

2 tbsp glucose syrup

150 g/5½ oz plain chocolate, roughly chopped

4 tbsp Scotch whisky

25 g/1 oz walnut pieces

1. Lightly brush a 20-cm/8-inch square baking tin with the oil. Line it with non-stick baking paper, snipping diagonally into the corners, then pressing the paper into the tin so that the base and sides are lined.

2. Put the sugar, butter, condensed milk and glucose syrup into a heavy-based saucepan. Heat gently, stirring constantly, until the sugar has dissolved.

3. Increase the heat and boil for 12–15 minutes, or until the mixture reaches 116°C/240°F on a sugar thermometer (if you don't have a sugar thermometer, spoon a little of the syrup into some iced water; it will form a soft ball when it is ready). As the temperature rises, stir the fudge occasionally so the sugar doesn't stick and burn. Remove the fudge from the heat. Add the chocolate and whisky and stir together until the chocolate has melted and the mixture is smooth.

4. Preheat the grill to medium-hot. Put the walnuts in a baking tray and toast them under the grill for 2–3 minutes, or until brown, then roughly chop.

5. Pour the mixture into the prepared tin, smooth the surface with a spatula and sprinkle over the walnuts. Leave to cool for 1 hour. Cover with clingfilm, then chill in the refrigerator for 1–2 hours, or until firm. Lift the fudge out of the tin, peel off the paper and cut into 16 squares. Store in an airtight container in a cool, dry place for up to 2 weeks.

CHOCOLATE TOFFEE
Popcorn

Planning a movie night in? Treat everyone with little individual bags of popcorn!

Prep: 10 mins, plus setting   Cook: 10–15 mins

Ingredients

1 tbsp sunflower oil, for oiling

2 tbsp sunflower oil

50 g/1¾ oz popping corn

40 g/1½ oz butter

40 g/1½ oz soft light brown sugar

40 g/1½ oz golden syrup

50 g/1¾ oz plain chocolate

100 g/3½ oz toffees, crushed

100 g/3½ oz plain chocolate chips

1. Lightly oil a large baking tray and two wooden spoons. Heat the oil in a large saucepan and add the corn. Cover with a lid and shake gently to coat with the oil.

2. Reduce the heat to low. Once you hear the corn popping pay attention to the speed of the pops – when it has reduced remove the pan from the heat.

3. Put the butter, sugar and golden syrup into a separate large saucepan and heat over a medium heat until the sugar has dissolved. Increase the heat and boil gently for 2 minutes.

4. Add the popcorn to the pan of toffee and use the prepared spoons to toss until evenly coated. Transfer to the prepared tray and leave to set.

5. Meanwhile, put the chocolate into a heatproof bowl set over a saucepan of gently simmering water and heat until melted.

6. Scatter the popcorn with the crushed toffees and chocolate chips and drizzle with the melted chocolate. Leave to set before serving. Store in a sealed container in a cool, dry place.

VARIATION
Want to speed things up? Use 50 g/1¾ oz popped corn instead of popping your own.

PEPPERMINT Creams

Makes 25

The pretty and tasty peppermint cream is an old-fashioned favourite. It's a refreshing choice for an after-dinner sweet.

Prep: 30 mins, plus setting   Cook: 5 mins

Ingredients

1 large egg white

325 g/11½ oz icing sugar, sifted

2–4 drops peppermint extract

2–4 drops green food colouring

10 g/¼ oz icing sugar, for dipping

100 g/3½ oz plain chocolate, roughly chopped

1. Line a baking tray with non-stick baking paper.

2. Lightly whisk the egg white in a large, clean mixing bowl until it is frothy but still translucent.

3. Add the sifted icing sugar to the egg white and stir with a wooden spoon until the mixture is stiff. Knead in the peppermint extract and food colouring.

4. Using the palms of your hands, roll the mixture into walnut-sized balls and place them on the prepared baking tray. Use a fork to flatten them; if it sticks to them, dip it in icing sugar before pressing. Put the creams in the refrigerator to set for 24 hours.

5. Put the chocolate in a heatproof bowl set over a saucepan of gently simmering water and heat until melted. Dip the creams halfway into the chocolate vertically and return to the baking tray for 1 hour, or until set. Store in an airtight container in the refrigerator for up to 5 days.

CHOCOLATE & HAZELNUT
Cake Balls

Makes 20

Creamy chocolate hazelnut spread and delicious chopped toasted hazelnuts give a smooth flavour and crunchy texture to these moreish little bites.

Prep: 30 mins, plus chilling   Cook: 30 mins, plus setting

Ingredients

2 eggs

50 g/1¾ oz soft light brown sugar

50 g/1¾ oz caster sugar

100 g/3½ oz plain flour, sifted

100 g/3½ oz butter, melted

1 tsp baking powder

2 tbsp cocoa powder, sifted

1 tsp vanilla extract

350 g/12 oz chocolate hazelnut spread

Decoration

350 g/12 oz plain chocolate, broken into pieces

70 g/2½ oz skinned whole hazelnuts

20 lollipop sticks or wooden skewers

1. Preheat the oven to 200°C/400°F/Gas Mark 6. Line an 18-cm/7-inch round cake tin and a baking tray with baking paper.

2. Place the eggs, brown sugar and caster sugar in a bowl and beat well until light and frothy.

3. Lightly fold in the flour, butter, baking powder, cocoa powder and vanilla extract. Leave to stand for 20 minutes. Pour into the prepared cake tin and bake in the preheated oven for 15–20 minutes, or until a skewer inserted in the middle of the cake comes out clean. Leave to cool in the tin for 10 minutes, then transfer to a wire rack to cool completely.

4. Use your fingertips to crumble the cooled cake into a mixing bowl. Stir in the chocolate hazelnut spread and mix together with a fork. Use an ice-cream scoop to remove a golf ball-sized piece of the mixture, then use your hands to shape it into a ball. Place on the prepared tray. Repeat with the remaining mixture to make 20 balls, then transfer to the refrigerator to chill for at least 30 minutes.

5. To make the decoration, put the chocolate into a heatproof bowl set over a saucepan of gently simmering water and heat until melted.

6. Place the hazelnuts in a dry frying pan and heat for 2–3 minutes, stirring constantly to prevent burning. Tip the toasted nuts onto a chopping board and roughly chop.

7. When ready to decorate the cake balls, insert a lollipop stick into each one and dip the cakes in the melted chocolate, using a teaspoon to help you to coat them completely. Return to the tray and sprinkle the top of each cake with hazelnuts. Transfer to a stand and leave to set.

CHOCOLATE & CARAMEL
Cups

If you don't have any petit four cases, line the holes in a mini muffin tin with small squares of clingfilm. Spread melted chocolate over it, then peel it away before serving.

Makes 12

Prep: 30 mins   Cook: 7–8 mins, plus chilling

Ingredients

150 g/5½ oz plain chocolate, roughly chopped

115 g/4 oz granulated sugar

4 tbsp water

12 small walnut halves

25 g/1 oz unsalted butter

125 ml/4 fl oz double cream

1. Line a 12-hole mini muffin tin with a double layer of paper petit four cases. Line a baking tray with non-stick baking paper.

2. Put the chocolate in a heatproof bowl, set the bowl over a saucepan of gently simmering water and heat until melted. Put a spoonful of melted chocolate into each paper case, then evenly brush over the sides using a small pastry brush. Chill in the refrigerator for 30 minutes, then brush on a second layer of chocolate, taking care over the sides so there is an even thickness. Cover and chill in the refrigerator.

3. Put the sugar and water into a small heavy-based saucepan. Heat gently for 5 minutes, or until the sugar has dissolved, tilting the pan to mix them together. Increase the heat and boil rapidly without stirring for 4–5 minutes, until the caramel is deep golden, taking care that it doesn't burn. Remove from the heat, add the walnuts, quickly coat them in the caramel, then lift them out using two forks. Put them on the prepared baking tray, spaced slightly apart.

4. Add the butter to the remaining caramel, tilt the pan to mix, then gradually stir in the cream. Transfer to a bowl, leave to cool, then cover and chill in the refrigerator for 1½ hours, or until thick. Lift the chocolate-lined paper cases out of the tin. Spoon the caramel cream into a large piping bag fitted with a large star nozzle and pipe it into the chocolate cups. Chill in the refrigerator until required. Decorate the cups with the caramel walnuts just before serving.

Chocolate 'Salami' Log

It's nice to have a little treat on hand when you have friends around. You'll be sneaking back to the fridge more than once for just a little more of this 'salami'.

Serves 12

Prep: 10 mins, plus chilling   Cook: 8 mins

Ingredients

75 g/2¾ oz blanched hazelnuts

40 g/1¼ oz flaked almonds

100 g/3½ oz dried figs, roughly chopped

2 tbsp triple sec

200 g/7 oz plain chocolate

75 g/2¾ oz butter

100 g/3½ oz soft light brown sugar

1 large egg, plus 1 large egg yolk

zest of 1 orange

200 g/7 oz amaretti biscuits

50 g/1¾ oz white chocolate chips

1 tbsp icing sugar, for dusting

1. Put the hazelnuts and almonds in a large, heavy-based frying pan and heat over a high heat, stirring frequently, until golden brown. Leave to cool slightly, then roughly chop.

2. Place the figs and triple sec in a microwave-proof bowl and heat on High for 1 minute. Set aside.

3. Put the chocolate and butter into a heatproof bowl set over a saucepan of gently simmering water and heat until melted.

4. Meanwhile, beat together the sugar, egg, egg yolk and orange zest in a separate bowl until thick and combined. Transfer to the chocolate mixture and stir for 5 minutes, or until the sugar is completely dissolved.

5. Crush the biscuits into smallish chunks and fold through the chocolate mixture with the figs, nuts and chocolate chips until evenly coated. Spoon the mixture onto a piece of greaseproof paper, shaping into a 20-cm/8-inch log. Tightly roll up the log, twisting both ends to secure. Chill in the refrigerator for 4 hours or overnight.

6. Remove from the refrigerator, dust with the icing sugar and serve. Store in the refrigerator.

VARIATION
Use your favourite
dried fruit and soak in
your preferred spirit
– rum, brandy or
amaretto.

DOUBLE CHOCOLATE
Pecan Blondies

Makes 12

With chunks of white and dark chocolate and crunchy pecan nuts, these moreish bars are an indulgent treat.

Prep: 30 mins, plus cooling   Cook: 35–40 mins

Ingredients

250 g/9 oz white chocolate, broken into pieces

40 g/1½ oz butter, plus extra for greasing

175 g/6 oz plain chocolate

2 large eggs, beaten

85 g/3 oz caster sugar

115 g/4 oz self-raising flour

100 g/3½ oz pecan nuts, roughly chopped

1. Preheat the oven to 180°C/350°F/Gas Mark 4. Grease a 20-cm/8-inch shallow square baking tin or baking dish.

2. Place 85 g/3 oz of the white chocolate and all the butter in a heatproof bowl set over a saucepan of gently simmering water and heat, stirring occasionally, until melted and smooth. Meanwhile, roughly chop the remaining white chocolate and plain chocolate.

3. Beat together the eggs and sugar in a large bowl, then stir in the melted chocolate mixture. Sift the flour over the top. Add the chopped chocolate and pecan nuts. Mix well.

4. Spoon the mixture into the prepared tin and smooth the surface. Bake in the preheated oven for 35–40 minutes, or until golden brown and just firm to the touch in the centre. Leave in the tin to cool completely, then turn out and cut into 12 bars.

TIP
Take care not to overcook the blondies or you'll lose that lovely soft, squidgy texture.

PLAIN CHOCOLATE &
Amaretto Truffles

Makes 12

These delectable morsels are so easy to make and look really glamorous!
Use any liqueur instead of the amaretto if you wish.

Prep: 30 mins, plus soaking and setting   Cook: 5–10 mins

Ingredients

50 ml/2 fl oz amaretto liqueur

55 g/2 oz sultanas

100 g/3½ oz plain chocolate,
roughly chopped

2 tbsp double cream

70 g/2½ oz ready-made
chocolate cake, crumbled

100 g/3½ oz hazelnuts

55 g/2 oz chocolate vermicelli,
to decorate

1. Put the amaretto and sultanas into a small mixing bowl, cover and leave to soak for 6–8 hours. Line a baking tray with non-stick baking paper.

2. Transfer the amaretto mixture to a food processor and whizz until puréed.

3. Put the chocolate and cream in a heatproof bowl set over a saucepan of gently simmering water and heat until the chocolate is melted. Remove from the heat, add the amaretto purée and chocolate cake and stir well.

4. When cool enough to handle, use the palms of your hands to roll the mixture into truffle-sized balls. Place them on the prepared tray.

5. Preheat the grill to medium. Put the hazelnuts on a baking tray and toast them under the grill for 2–3 minutes, or until brown, shaking them halfway through. Finely chop them.

6. Spread the chocolate vermicelli on one plate and scatter the hazelnuts on another. Roll half the truffles in the vermicelli and half in the hazelnuts.

7. Return to the tray, cover with non-stick baking paper and chill in the refrigerator for 1–2 hours, or until firm. Store in an airtight container in the refrigerator for up to 5 days.

SOFT

HOT CHOCOLATE FUDGE
Layer Cake

Serves 8

With a super-speedy whisked sponge, a tub of ready-made fudge frosting and some whipped cream you really can create a rich and indulgent chocolate cake in 30 minutes!

Prep: 30 mins, plus cooling   Cook: 12–15 mins

Ingredients

10 g/¼ oz butter, for greasing

3 eggs

85 g/3 oz caster sugar

85 g/3 oz plain flour

2 tbsp cocoa powder

10 g/¼ oz caster sugar, for dusting

200 ml/7 fl oz double cream

225 g/8 oz ready-made chocolate fudge frosting

plain and white chocolate flakes or curls, to decorate (optional)

10 g/¼ oz cocoa powder, for dusting

1. Preheat the oven to 200°C/400°F/Gas Mark 6. Lightly grease a 23-cm x 33-cm/9 x 13-inch Swiss roll tin and line the base and sides with baking paper.

2. Put the eggs and sugar into a large bowl set over a saucepan of gently simmering water. Beat with a hand-held electric mixer for 3–4 minutes, or until the mixture is very thick and pale.

3. Sift in the flour and cocoa powder and gently fold in. Pour into the prepared tin and level the surface. Bake in the preheated oven for 8–10 minutes, or until risen and springy to the touch. Meanwhile, dust a sheet of baking paper with caster sugar and whip the cream until it holds firm peaks.

4. Remove the cake from the oven and immediately turn out onto the prepared baking paper. Cut the cake into three strips and transfer to a wire rack to cool for 5–8 minutes.

5. Spread the frosting over the top of each strip and sandwich the strips together with the cream. Decorate with the chocolate flakes, if using, and dust with the cocoa powder.

TIP
The beaten mixture should be thick enough to leave a ribbon-like trail on the surface when the beaters are lifted.

CHILLI & CHOCOLATE
Churros

Makes 16

Chilli and chocolate are frequently used together in South American cooking and are a surprisingly good flavour combination.

Prep: 20 mins, plus cooling   Cook: 25 mins

Ingredients

100 g/3½ oz unsalted butter, diced

225 ml/8 fl oz water

140 g/5 oz plain flour, sifted

large pinch of salt

2 large eggs, beaten

½ small red chilli, deseeded and very finely chopped

oil, for deep-frying

4 tbsp sugar

2 tsp cocoa powder, sifted

Chocolate Sauce

85 g/3 oz plain chocolate, broken into pieces

100 ml/3½ fl oz double cream

½ tsp vanilla extract

1 tsp dried chilli flakes, crushed

1. To make the chocolate sauce, put the chocolate and cream into a heatproof bowl set over a saucepan of gently simmering water and heat until the chocolate is melted. Remove from the heat and stir until smooth, then stir in the vanilla extract and chilli flakes. Set aside and keep warm.

2. Put the butter and water into a large saucepan over a low heat and heat until the butter has melted. Bring to the boil, remove from the heat and tip in the flour and salt. Beat thoroughly until the mixture is smooth and comes away from the side of the pan. Leave to cool for 5 minutes, then gradually beat in the eggs to make a thick and glossy paste. Beat in the chilli.

3. Heat enough oil for deep-frying in a large saucepan or deep-fryer to 180–190°C/350–375°F, or until a cube of bread browns in 30 seconds. Spoon the paste into a large piping bag fitted with a large star nozzle and pipe four 10-cm/4-inch lengths of the paste into the hot oil. Fry for 2–3 minutes, turning frequently, until crisp and golden. Remove with a slotted spoon and drain on kitchen paper. Keep warm while frying the remaining mixture.

4. Mix together the sugar and cocoa powder on a flat plate and toss the warm churros in the mixture in batches to coat. Serve immediately with the chocolate sauce for dipping.

TIP
Plain chocolate has more cacao and less sugar than other chocolates, so it is healthier than milk and white chocolate.

Molten Marshmallow
Chocolate Chunk Brownies

Makes 12

Brownies just got even better! Chocolate and marshmallow are perfectly paired in this gorgeous gooey mess!

Prep: 20 mins, plus cooling   Cook: 25 mins

Ingredients

10 g/¼ oz unsalted butter, for greasing

250 g/9 oz unsalted butter

250 g/9 oz plain chocolate

4 large eggs

350 g/12 oz caster sugar

½ tbsp vanilla extract

½ tsp salt

150 g/5½ oz plain flour

75 g/2¾ oz large chocolate buttons or chocolate chunks

75 g/2¾ oz marshmallow fluff

1. Preheat the oven to 180°C/350°F/Gas Mark 4. Grease a 22-cm/8½-inch square baking tin and line with baking paper.

2. Put the butter and chocolate into a heatproof bowl set over a saucepan of gently simmering water and heat, stirring occasionally, until melted. Remove from the heat and leave to cool slightly. Beat together the eggs, sugar, vanilla extract and salt in a bowl or jug.

3. Beat the egg mixture into the cooled chocolate mixture, then fold in the flour. Stir in half the chocolate buttons, pour into the prepared tin and bake in the preheated oven for 30 minutes.

4. Carefully remove the brownie from the oven (do not switch off the oven) and add spoonfuls of the marshmallow fluff to the top.

5. Scatter with the remaining chocolate buttons and bake for a further 10–15 minutes until the marshmallow is molten and beginning to colour. Leave to cool slightly, then cut into 12 squares and serve.

VARIATION

If you can't get marshmallow fluff, you could use 75 g/2¾ oz white marshmallows instead.

CHOCOLATE & SAFFRON
Brioches

Makes 12

Saffron will add a subtle and sophisticated flavour to your baking. It's also said to have aphrodisiac qualities, so these brioches would be perfect for a Valentine's Day brunch!

Prep: 35 mins, plus proving and cooling   Cook: 45 mins

Ingredients

pinch of saffron threads

3 tbsp boiling water

10 g/¼ oz melted butter, for greasing

55 g/2 oz butter, melted

350 g/12 oz plain flour

pinch of salt

1 tbsp caster sugar

2½ tsp easy-blend dried yeast

2 eggs, beaten

6 squares plain chocolate, halved, 30 g/1 oz in total

1 tbsp milk, for glazing

1. Add the saffron to the boiling water and leave to cool completely.

2. Lightly brush 12 individual brioche tins or fluted patty tins with melted butter.

3. Sift together the flour, salt and sugar into a bowl and stir in the yeast. Add the saffron liquid, eggs and butter and stir to make a soft dough.

4. Knead until smooth, then cover and leave to stand in a warm place for 1–1½ hours, until doubled in size. Knead briefly, then shape three quarters of the dough into 12 balls. Place one in every tin and press a piece of chocolate firmly into each.

5. Shape the remaining dough into small balls with a pointed end. Brush with milk and press the balls into each brioche, sealing well.

6. Cover with oiled clingfilm and leave to stand in a warm place for 1½ hours, or until doubled in size. Meanwhile, preheat the oven to 200°C/400°F/Gas Mark 6. Brush the brioches with the milk and bake in the preheated oven for 12–15 minutes, until firm and golden. Turn out and serve warm.

TIP
If you don't have a pestle and mortar, place the peppercorns in a polythene bag and crush them with a rolling pin.

Pink Peppercorn &
Chocolate Cupcakes

Makes 12

Pepper with chocolate is a surprising combination, but it works! Here, the crushed pink peppercorns provide lovely colour contrast as well as flavour.

Prep: 35 mins, plus cooling   Cook: 25 mins

Ingredients

125 g/4½ oz plain flour

60 g/2¼ oz cocoa powder

1 tsp baking powder

¼ tsp salt

115 g/4 oz unsalted butter, softened

200 g/7 oz caster sugar

2 tsp vanilla extract

2 large eggs

125 ml/4 fl oz soured cream

1 tbsp pink peppercorns, crushed, to decorate

Frosting

4 tbsp milk

1 tbsp pink peppercorns, crushed

115 g/4 oz unsalted butter, softened

250 g/9 oz icing sugar

2 tsp vanilla extract

1. Preheat the oven to 180°C/350°F/Gas Mark 4 and line a 12-hole cupcake tin with paper cases.

2. Sift together the flour, cocoa powder, baking powder and salt into a bowl. Put the butter and caster sugar into a separate bowl and beat until pale and fluffy. Add the vanilla extract, then add the eggs, one at a time, beating after each addition. Add half of the flour mixture and the soured cream and beat until combined. Add the remaining flour mixture and mix.

3. Spoon the batter into the paper cases and bake in the preheated oven for 20 minutes, until risen and a cocktail stick inserted into the centre of a cupcake comes out clean. Leave to cool in the tin for 1–2 minutes, then transfer to a wire rack to cool completely.

4. Meanwhile, to make the frosting, put the milk and peppercorns into a small saucepan and heat over a medium heat until just boiling. Reduce the heat to low and simmer for about 5 minutes, stirring frequently. Strain the milk into a bowl, discarding the peppercorns, and leave to cool for about 10 minutes.

5. Add the butter, icing sugar and vanilla extract to the milk and beat with a hand-held electric mixer until well combined. Add more icing sugar, if necessary, to achieve a piping consistency. Spoon the frosting into a piping bag fitted with a star-shaped nozzle and pipe onto the cupcakes.

6. To decorate, sprinkle a little of the crushed pink peppercorns over the tops of the cupcakes.

MINI CHOCOLATE
Whoopie Pies

Who would have thought you could make these treats in such a short time? For a special occasion replace the chocolate spread with whipped cream and jam.

Makes 22

Prep: 20 mins, plus cooling and chilling   Cook: 8 mins

Ingredients

100 g/3½ oz butter, softened

125 g/4½ oz dark muscovado sugar

1 egg, lightly beaten

½ tsp vanilla extract

175 g/6 oz self-raising flour

25 g/1 oz cocoa powder

5 tbsp milk

4–5 tbsp chocolate hazelnut spread

1. Preheat the oven to 190°C/375°F/Gas Mark 5. Line two large baking sheets with baking paper.

2. Put the butter and sugar into a large bowl and beat with a hand-held electric mixer for 1–2 minutes. Whisk in the egg and vanilla extract. Sift in the flour and cocoa powder, add the milk and gently fold in until thoroughly combined.

3. Pipe or spoon 44 small mounds of the mixture onto the prepared baking sheet. Each mound should be about 4 cm/1½ inches in diameter. Bake in the preheated oven for 7–8 minutes, or until just firm. Carefully transfer the hot cakes to a wire rack using a palette knife. Leave to cool for 10 minutes.

4. Sandwich the cakes together with the chocolate hazelnut spread. If the spread starts to soften because the cakes are still slightly warm, pop the filled whoopie pies in the refrigerator for a few minutes until completely cold.

TIP
To speed up the cooling process gently flip the cakes over on the rack after 5 minutes.

WHITE CHOCOLATE & Blackberry Muffins

Makes 12

Muffins are so simple to make. Why not whip up a batch tonight and slip one into everyone's lunch box for a treat tomorrow!

Prep: 10–15 mins   Cook: 25–30 mins

Ingredients

300 g/10½ oz plain flour

1 tsp baking powder

200 g/7 oz caster sugar

100 g/3½ oz unsalted butter

2 eggs

1 tbsp vanilla extract

250 ml/9 fl oz low-fat natural yogurt

200 g/7 oz blackberries

200 g/7 oz white chocolate, chopped into chunks

1. Preheat the oven to 180°C/350°F/Gas Mark 4. Line a 12-hole muffin tin with paper cases.

2. Sift together the flour, baking powder and sugar into a large bowl. In a separate bowl beat together the butter, eggs, vanilla extract and yogurt until combined.

3. Fold the egg mixture into the flour mixture until just combined. Stir in the blackberries and chocolate.

4. Spoon the mixture evenly into the paper cases and bake in the preheated oven for 25–30 minutes until golden and cooked through. The muffins should bounce back when pressed gently with a finger. Transfer to a wire rack to cool.

TIP
The secret of a good muffin is not to over-mix. It's fine if some flour is still showing when you put them in the oven.

CHUNKY CHOCOLATE
Bread & Butter Pudding

Lift your bread and butter pudding into the realms of luxury with the addition of dark chocolate and sweet dried figs. Serve with a little cream for a real treat.

Prep: 10 mins, plus cooling   Cook: 35–40 mins

Ingredients

1 large brioche loaf

200 g/7 oz butter, softened

150 g/5½ plain chocolate, 70% cocoa solids, broken into large pieces

100 g/3½ oz chopped dried figs

4 large eggs

600 ml/1 pint milk

150 g/5½ oz caster sugar

1 tsp vanilla extract

1. Preheat the oven to 160°C/325°F/Gas Mark 3.

2. Line a 900-g/2-lb loaf tin with baking paper.

3. Slice the brioche and butter each slice on one side. Sprinkle the chocolate and figs over the buttered side of the slices. Put the slices back into the shape of the loaf and fit it into the prepared tin.

4. In a medium-sized bowl whisk together the eggs, milk, sugar and vanilla extract, then pour the mixture over the brioche and leave to soak for 5 minutes.

5. Bake in the preheated oven for 35–40 minutes, or until golden and the juices have set in the middle. Remove from the oven and leave to cool for 10 minutes before serving.

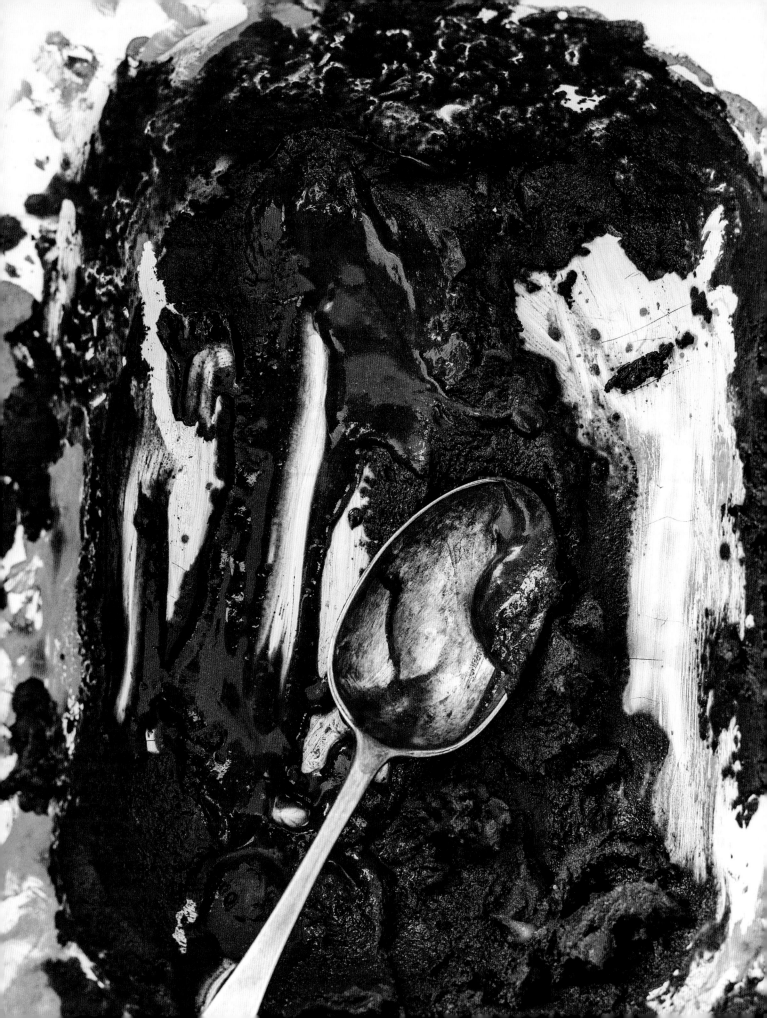

SOFT

When you bake or decorate with chocolate, the better the raw materials, the better the result.

Chocolate for cooking

Good-quality plain chocolate has an intense flavour and rich dark colour that are ideal for desserts and cakes. Milk and white chocolate are less intense in flavour but are useful for creating contrasting colour.

Couverture chocolate

The king of cooking chocolate, this has a very high cocoa butter content, so it melts smoothly and forms a thin crisp coating when tempered and cooled. Couverture chocolate is used mainly for moulding and coating hand-made chocolates.

Buttons and chips

These keep their shape when baked, and they also melt easily and evenly into batters and doughs, so you don't need to chop up a chocolate bar into uneven chunks. They contain less cocoa butter than bars, but they're ideal for using in cakes and chocolate chip cookies.

Cake covering chocolate

Easier to melt and handle than plain chocolate, this works well for decorations and for coating cakes. The disadvantage is that some or all of the cocoa butter has been replaced by other fats, such as coconut oil or palm oil, so the taste and texture aren't as refined as those of chocolate bars.

Cocoa powder

Not to be confused with sweetened drinking chocolate, cocoa is probably the most economical way of giving cakes and desserts a good chocolate flavour.

How to melt

When you use chocolate in cakes and desserts, it usually needs melting. Like mayonnaise, chocolate is basically an emulsion of different liquids that will separate if mistreated. If you melt it at too high a heat, it will 'seize' (split), go grainy or even burn. Along with heat, water is an enemy too. A single drop or even a puff of steam will cause seizing, so make sure your saucepan and utensils are absolutely dry.

In the microwave

Dark chocolate: microwave on Medium for about 2 minutes.
Milk and white chocolate: microwave on Low for about 2 minutes.
The chocolate will not change shape but will start to look shiny. Check and stir every 30 seconds.

In a very low oven

Preheat the oven to 110°C/225°F/Gas Mark ¼. Chop the chocolate, put it in an ovenproof bowl and heat in the oven for a few minutes. Remove before completely melted and stir until smooth.

Over simmering water

Chop the chocolate into small pieces so that it melts quickly and evenly. Put it into a dry, heatproof bowl set over a saucepan of gently simmering water, making sure the base of the bowl isn't touching the water. The bowl should fit really snugly over the saucepan so that steam can't escape and make the chocolate seize. Heat gently, stirring occasionally, until smooth.

Over direct heat

This can be done only if the recipe includes a heated liquid such as milk or cream. The heat of the liquid protects the chocolate and helps to melt it. Gently heat the liquid in a heavy-based saucepan over a low heat. Stir in the chopped chocolate, then stir until smooth. Immediately remove from the heat.

White Chocolate & Passion Fruit Éclairs

Makes 10

These light, fruity éclairs with their white chocolate topping look delicious and have a distinctly tropical flavour – perfect for summer occasions.

Prep: 30 mins, plus cooling and standing   Cook: 45 mins

Ingredients

50 g/1¾ oz butter

150 ml/5 fl oz cold water

60 g/2¼ oz plain flour, sifted

pinch of salt

2 large eggs, beaten

200 ml/7 fl oz double cream

2 passion fruit

Topping

200 g/7 oz white chocolate, broken into pieces

yellow writing icing (optional)

1. Preheat the oven to 200°C/400°F/Gas Mark 6. Line two baking trays with baking paper.

2. Place the butter and water in a medium-sized saucepan and bring to the boil. Add the flour and salt and beat well until the mixture starts to come away from the side of the pan. Remove from the heat and leave to cool for 1–2 minutes.

3. Gradually beat in the eggs until the mixture is smooth and glossy. Transfer to a piping bag fitted with a 2.5-cm/1-inch nozzle and pipe ten 8-cm/3¼-inch lengths of the mixture onto the prepared trays.

4. Bake in the preheated oven for 15 minutes, then remove from the oven and use a fine skewer to make a slit along the length of each éclair to allow the steam to escape. Return to the oven and bake for a further 10 minutes, then transfer to a wire rack to cool.

5. Whip the cream until it just holds stiff peaks. Cut the passion fruit in half and use a teaspoon to remove the flesh. Stir into the cream and use either a piping bag or a teaspoon to fill the éclairs with the mixture.

6. To make the topping, place the chocolate in a heatproof bowl set over a saucepan of gently simmering water and heat until melted. Use a teaspoon to spread the melted chocolate evenly over the filled éclairs. To create a feathered effect, pipe 2–3 straight lines lengthways on the chocolate with the writing icing, if using. Carefully drag a cocktail stick backwards and forwards across the lines at regular intervals. Leave to stand for 30 minutes before serving.

CHOCOLATE CAKE
Doughnuts

Makes 14

These delicious doughnuts are made without yeast, so they're much quicker to prepare than normal doughnuts and you'll get them to the table faster.

Prep: 25 mins, plus resting   Cook: 55 mins

Ingredients

125 ml/4 fl oz lukewarm milk

1 egg

1 tsp vanilla extract

30 g/1 oz cocoa powder

225 g/8 oz plain flour

½ tsp bicarbonate of soda

½ tsp baking powder

½ tsp salt

100 g/3½ oz caster sugar

25 g/1 oz butter

10 g/¼ oz flour, for dusting

oil, for deep-frying

Glaze

40 g/1½ oz plain chocolate, broken into pieces

40 g/1½ oz white chocolate, broken into pieces

1. Blend together the milk, egg and vanilla extract in a bowl.

2. Using a stand mixer with a paddle attachment, mix the cocoa powder, flour, bicarbonate of soda, baking powder, salt and sugar together. Add the butter and blend. Slowly add the milk, egg and vanilla mixture. Mix until the batter is smooth and thick and resembles a biscuit dough.

3. Leave the dough to rest in the mixer for 20 minutes.

4. Turn out the dough out on a floured work surface and roll out to a thickness of 1 cm/½ inch. Use a doughnut cutter to stamp out 14 doughnuts.

5. Heat enough oil for deep-frying in a large saucepan or deep-fryer to 180–190°C/350–375°F, or until a cube of bread browns in 30 seconds. Carefully place the doughnuts, one at a time, into the oil. Fry for 2 minutes on each side, or until golden brown. Remove with a slotted spoon and drain on kitchen paper.

6. To make the glaze, place the plain chocolate and white chocolate in separate heatproof bowls set over saucepans of gently simmering water and heat until melted. Use the plain chocolate to coat 7 doughnuts and the white chocolate to coat the remaining doughnuts, drizzling a contrasting pattern over the coating when set.

VARIATION
You could replace the plain and white chocolate with milk chocolate, if you prefer.

TIP
When adding the egg
whites to the melted
chocolate, beat them
in quickly so that the
chocolate doesn't
seize.

CHOCOLATE MOUSSE
Brownie Layered Puddings

Show off these trendy little layered puddings by serving them in straight glasses. They will look spectacular and are bound to impress.

Makes
4

Prep: 30 mins, plus chilling   Cook: 5 mins

Ingredients

120 g/4¼ oz white chocolate,
finely chopped

4 large egg whites

2 tbsp caster sugar

4 x 100 g/3½ oz brownie
squares

8 tbsp dulce de leche
(caramel sauce)

100 ml/3½ fl oz double cream

1 tsp cocoa powder, to decorate

1. Put the chocolate into a heatproof bowl set over a saucepan of gently simmering water and heat until melted.

2. Whisk the egg whites in a grease-free bowl until they hold soft peaks. Add the sugar and whisk until they hold firm peaks.

3. Spoon one third of the egg whites into the melted chocolate and beat in. Using a large metal spoon gently fold in the remaining egg whites until well combined.

4. Trim the brownies into rounds that will fit snugly in the glasses, reserving the trimmings. Slice the brownies in half horizontally.

5. Divide half the chocolate mousse mixture between four small straight-sided jars or glasses. Carefully top each with a slice of brownie, then drizzle over 1 tablespoon of the dulce de leche. Work carefully, defining the layers. Repeat the layers once more.

6. Lightly whip the cream and spoon it over the layered puddings. Crumble over the reserved brownie trimmings and sprinkle with a pinch of cocoa powder. Transfer to the refrigerator for 4 hours or overnight to chill and set.

Cocoa & Cinnamon
Madeleines with White Chocolate

Makes 12

These distinctive shell-shaped cakes are quintessentially French. These chocolate-dipped ones may not be traditional, but are definitely delicious!

Prep: 30 mins, plus standing and cooling   Cook: 15 mins

Ingredients

10 g/¼ oz melted butter, for greasing

10 g/¼ oz flour, for dusting

2 eggs

50 g/1¾ oz soft light brown sugar

50 g/1¾ oz caster sugar

100 g/3½ oz plain flour, sifted

100 g/3½ oz butter, melted

1 tsp baking powder

½ tsp ground cinnamon

2 tbsp cocoa powder, sifted

1 tsp vanilla extract

100 g/3½ oz white chocolate, broken into pieces, to decorate

1. Preheat the oven to 200°C/400°F/Gas Mark 6. Lightly grease a 12-hole madeleine tin and dust with flour.

2. Place the eggs, brown sugar and caster sugar in a mixing bowl and beat well until the mixture is light and frothy.

3. Lightly fold in the flour, butter, baking powder, cinnamon, cocoa powder and vanilla extract. Leave to stand for 20 minutes.

4. Divide the mixture between the holes in the prepared tin and bake in the preheated oven for 8–10 minutes until well risen. Leave to cool in the tin for 1–2 minutes, then transfer to a wire rack to cool completely.

5. To decorate, place the chocolate in a heatproof bowl set over a saucepan of gently simmering water and heat until melted. Dip the end of each madeleine in the melted chocolate and leave to set on a baking sheet. Eat on the day of making.

PAIN-AU-CHOCOLAT
Cinnamon Rolls

Makes 12

Can't decide between a sweet cinnamon roll or a crisp and flaky pain au chocolat? Well, now you can enjoy the best of both with this delicious quick-and-easy hybrid of the two!

Prep: 20 mins, plus standing, chilling and cooling   Cook: 15–20 mins

Ingredients

100 g/3½ oz plain chocolate, broken into pieces

320 g/11 oz ready-rolled puff pastry

25 g/1 oz unsalted butter, melted

2 tbsp caster sugar

1½ tsp ground cinnamon

10 g/¼ oz icing sugar, for dusting

1. Put the chocolate into a heatproof bowl set over a saucepan of gently simmering water and heat until melted. Remove from the heat, stir until smooth, then leave to cool for 15 minutes, stirring occasionally.

2. Unroll the sheet of puff pastry and place on a board. Generously brush with some of the melted butter. Leave to stand for 10 minutes, then spread the cooled chocolate all over the buttered pastry. Mix together the sugar and cinnamon in a bowl, then sprinkle over the chocolate.

3. Roll up the pastry, Swiss roll-style, from one long side then brush all over with more of the melted butter. Chill in the refrigerator for 15 minutes. Preheat the oven to 220°C/425°F/Gas Mark 7. Use the remaining melted butter to grease a 12-hole cupcake tin.

4. Using a serrated knife, slice the pastry roll into 12 even-sized rounds. Place each round in a hole in the prepared cupcake tin.

5. Bake in the preheated oven for 15–20 minutes, or until risen and golden brown. Leave to cool in the tin for 5 minutes, then transfer to a wire rack. Dust the rolls with icing sugar and serve warm or cold.

VARIATION
For a mocha-flavoured filling, replace the cinnamon with 2 teaspoons of instant coffee powder.

WHITE CHOCOLATE
Blondies

Makes 12

For a morning coffee treat, these soft, squidgy blondies are hard to beat. Mixed in one bowl and baked in under 25 minutes, they are the perfect speedy bake!

Prep: 15 mins, plus cooling   Cook: 22 mins

Ingredients

10 g/¼ oz butter, for greasing

115 g/4 oz butter

225 g/8 oz light muscovado sugar

2 eggs

1 tsp vanilla extract

150 g/5½ oz plain flour

pinch of salt

85 g/3 oz white chocolate chips

1. Preheat the oven to 200°C/400°F/Gas Mark 6. Lightly grease a 20-cm/8-inch shallow square cake tin and line with baking paper.

2. Put the butter into a small saucepan and melt over a low heat. Transfer to a large bowl with the sugar, then beat with a balloon whisk until combined.

3. Beat in the eggs and vanilla extract, then sift in the flour and salt and beat well until smooth. Pour the mixture into the prepared tin and level the surface with a spatula. Scatter over the chocolate chips.

4. Bake in the preheated oven for 20–22 minutes, or until golden brown and just set (the centre will still be a little soft). Leave to cool in the tin, then turn out and cut into 12 squares.

TIP
To save time, use a microwave-proof mixing bowl and melt the butter on High for 20-30 seconds.

CHOCOLATE-SWIRLED
Pumpkin Pie Slice

Serves 16

Pumpkin pie is an American classic made all the better with a luxurious swirl of dark chocolate!

Prep: 25 mins, plus chilling   Cook: 1 hour

Ingredients

10 g/¼ oz butter, for greasing

250 g/9 oz digestive biscuits

200 g/7 oz plain chocolate

50 g/1¾ oz unsalted butter, melted

400 g/14 oz cream cheese

400 g/14 oz caster sugar

400 g/14 oz canned solid pumpkin purée

3 large eggs

1 tsp vanilla extract

40 g/1½ oz plain flour

1 tsp ground cinnamon

½ tsp salt

1. Preheat the oven to 180°C/350°F/Gas Mark 4. Grease a 24-cm/10-inch square baking tin and line with baking paper. Place the biscuits in a food processor bowl and pulse until you have coarse crumbs.

2. Put 75 g/2¾ oz of the chocolate into a heatproof bowl set over a saucepan of gently simmering water and heat until melted. Add the butter and the melted chocolate to the biscuit crumbs and pulse to combine. Transfer to the prepared tin and press in firmly with the back of a spoon. Bake in the preheated oven for 12–15 minutes, then remove from the oven and leave to cool (do not switch off the oven).

3. Place the cream cheese in a bowl and lightly whisk until smooth. Add the sugar, pumpkin purée, eggs, vanilla extract, flour, cinnamon and salt. Lightly whisk until the mixture is smooth and combined.

4. Put the remaining chocolate into a heatproof bowl set over a saucepan of gently simmering water and heat until melted. Remove from the heat and add about 200 g/7 oz of the pumpkin mixture, stirring well to combine.

5. Pour the remaining pumpkin mixture into the prepared tin. Place large spoonfuls of the chocolate pumpkin mixture on the pumpkin mixture, then drag a knife through to create swirls.

6. Transfer to the oven and bake for 40–45 minutes. The pie should still have a slight wobble in the centre. Leave to cool to room temperature, then wrap in clingfilm and chill in the refrigerator for 2 hours or overnight until firm. Cut into 16 slices and serve.

ZEBRA PUDDINGS WITH
Hot Chocolate Fudge Sauce

Makes 6

These lovely marbled puddings make a luxurious dessert after a special meal. You could use milk or white chocolate in the sauce if you prefer.

Prep: 40 mins   Cook: 30 mins

Ingredients

1 tbsp vegetable oil, for oiling

10 g/¼ oz flour, for dusting

125 ml/4 fl oz vegetable oil

125 g/4½ oz caster sugar

4 tbsp milk

2 eggs, beaten

150 g/5½ oz self-raising flour, sifted

½ tsp baking powder

15 g/½ oz cocoa powder, sifted

Sauce

300 ml/10 fl oz double cream

200 g/7 oz plain chocolate, chopped

1 tbsp golden syrup

25 g/1 oz butter

1. Lightly oil six 175-ml/6-fl oz dariole moulds or ramekin dishes and dust with flour. Preheat the oven to 180°C/350°F/Gas Mark 4.

2. Place the oil, sugar, milk and eggs in a mixing bowl and gently whisk to combine. Divide the mixture between two bowls.

3. Add 100 g/3½ oz of the flour and half the baking powder to one of the bowls and fold to combine. Add the remaining flour and baking powder together with the cocoa powder to the other bowl and mix well. Make sure that both mixtures have the same consistency; they should be pourable but not runny. If they need to be looser, add a little more milk.

4. Begin to build the sponge mixtures in the moulds. Pour a little of the vanilla mixture into each of the moulds to cover the base. Pour a little of the chocolate mixture into the centre of each, then repeat with the vanilla mixture. Alternate and repeat until all the mixture has been used, always pouring into the centre to form a 'zebra' pattern. Place the moulds on a baking tray and bake in the preheated oven for 20–25 minutes, until well risen and a skewer inserted in the middle of the cakes comes out clean. Leave in the moulds until ready to serve.

5. Meanwhile, make the sauce. Heat the cream in a saucepan to just below boiling point. Stir in the chocolate, golden syrup and butter and gently mix until the chocolate has melted and combined with the other ingredients. The sauce should be smooth and glossy.

6. Remove the puddings from the moulds, pour the sauce over and serve immediately.

CHOCOLATE POLENTA
Cake

Serves 6

A scoop of vanilla ice cream or tangy crème fraîche and a few fresh berries will turn this wonderfully moist and crumbly chocolate cake into a heavenly dinner party dessert.

Prep: 15 mins   Cook: 15–20 mins

Ingredients

10 g/¼ oz butter, for greasing

85 g/3 oz self-raising flour

25 g/1 oz cocoa powder

55 g/2 oz quick-cook polenta

115 g/4 oz butter, softened

115 g/4 oz caster sugar

2 large eggs

10 g/¼ oz cocoa powder, for dusting

ready-made chocolate sauce, to serve (optional)

1. Preheat the oven to 200°C/400°F/Gas Mark 6. Grease a 20-cm/8-inch round shallow cake tin and line the base with baking paper. Sift together the flour and cocoa powder into a large bowl and add the polenta, butter, sugar and eggs. Beat with a hand-held electric mixer for 1–2 minutes until combined.

2. Spoon the mixture into the prepared tin and gently level the surface. Bake in the preheated oven for 15–20 minutes, or until risen and just firm to the touch.

3. Carefully turn out the cake onto a wire rack. Serve warm or cold, cut into thin slices (allow 2 slices per person), dusted with cocoa powder and drizzled with chocolate sauce, if using.

VARIATION

To make a lemon polenta cake, replace the cocoa powder with 25 g/1 oz self-raising flour and add the grated rind and juice of 1 lemon. Bake for 18–24 minutes.

MELT

CHOCOLATE MOUSSE
with a Chilli Kick

Serves 4

These heavenly little desserts have a good undertone of dark rum, zingy orange and delicious sour cherries, as well as the unexpected chilli kick.

Prep: 20 mins, plus cooling and setting   Cook: 5 mins

Ingredients

150 g/5½ oz plain chocolate, 70% cocoa solids, broken into pieces

pinch of salt

4 large eggs, separated

55 g/2 oz caster sugar

150 ml/5 fl oz double cream

1 tsp chipotle powder

2 tsp orange zest

100 g/3½ oz sour cherries

100 ml/3½ fl oz dark rum

55 g/2 oz roasted hazelnuts

1. Place the chocolate pieces in a large heatproof bowl set over a saucepan of gently simmering water and heat, stirring occasionally, until melted. Remove from the heat and set aside until cool.

2. Beat the salt, egg yolks and sugar into the cooled chocolate.

3. In a separate bowl whip the cream until it has thickened slightly.

4. Put the egg whites into a clean grease-free bowl and whisk until they hold stiff peaks.

5. Add the chipotle powder and 1 teaspoon of the orange zest to the chocolate mixture, then fold in the cream, followed by the egg whites. Divide between four glasses and place in the refrigerator for 2 hours to set.

6. Meanwhile, soak the sour cherries in the rum and roughly chop the hazelnuts.

7. Just before serving, remove the mousse from the refrigerator and top with the rum-soaked sour cherries, the hazelnuts and the remaining orange zest.

LEMON & WHITE
Chocolate Creams

For an Asian twist on these decadent truffles, add a large pinch of ground cardamom seeds and star anise to the cream and chocolate mixture.

Prep: 40 mins, plus setting   Cook: 5–10 mins

Ingredients

300 g/10½ oz white chocolate, roughly chopped

2 tbsp double cream

finely grated rind of 1 lemon

2 tbsp limoncello

55 g/2 oz unsalted butter, softened and diced

25 g/1 oz pistachio nuts, finely chopped

1. Put 100 g/3½ oz of the chocolate and all the cream into a heatproof bowl set over a saucepan of gently simmering water and heat until the chocolate is melted.

2. Remove from the heat, add the lemon rind, limoncello and butter and whisk for 3–4 minutes, or until thickened. Transfer to an airtight container and chill in the refrigerator for 6–8 hours, or until firm.

3. Line a baking tray with non-stick baking paper. Scoop teaspoonfuls of the mixture and, using the palms of your hands, roll them into 12 truffle-sized balls. Place the balls on the prepared tray, cover with clingfilm and freeze for 6–8 hours.

4. Put the remaining chocolate in a heatproof bowl set over a saucepan of gently simmering water and heat until melted.

5. Using two forks, dip each truffle into the chocolate to coat evenly. Return to the tray, sprinkle over the pistachio nuts and chill in the refrigerator for 1–2 hours, or until firm. Store in an airtight container in the refrigerator for up to 5 days.

S'MORES
Semifreddo

Semifreddo is an easy-to-slice ice cream that looks very impressive and tastes divine. It's a perfect get-ahead dessert for any dinner party or occasion.

Prep: 40 mins, plus chilling   Cook: 10 mins

Ingredients

1 tsp vegetable oil, for oiling

100 g/3½ oz plain chocolate

4 large eggs, separated

100 g/3½ oz caster sugar

300 ml/10 fl oz double cream

200 g/7 oz digestive biscuits, crumbled, plus 1 biscuit to decorate

150 g/5½ oz dulce de leche (caramel sauce)

75 g/2¾ oz white mini marshmallows

½ tsp water

1. Oil a 900-g/2-lb loaf tin and line with clingfilm. Put half the chocolate into a heatproof bowl set over a saucepan of gently simmering water and heat until melted. Remove from the heat.

2. Put the egg yolks and sugar in a separate bowl and whisk until they leave a trail when the whisk is lifted.

3. Put the egg whites into a clean, grease-free bowl and whisk until they hold stiff peaks. Pour the cream into a separate bowl and whip until it holds soft peaks.

4. Using a large metal spoon fold the cream into the egg yolk mixture, then fold in the melted chocolate and, finally, carefully fold in the egg whites. Spoon one third of the mixture into the prepared tin, then scatter over half the crumbled biscuits. Drizzle over half the dulce de leche, then repeat once before topping with the remaining egg mixture. Wrap with clingfilm and transfer to the freezer for at least 6 hours until firm.

5. To serve, remove from the freezer and set aside while you prepare the toppings. Put the remaining chocolate into a heatproof bowl set over a saucepan of gently simmering water and heat until melted.

6. Put 50 g/1¾ oz of the marshmallows in the microwave with the water and heat for 10–15 seconds on Low. Mix together until smooth and thick but still runny.

7. Remove the clingfilm from the semifreddo and turn out onto a plate. Spoon over the melted marshmallow and allow to dribble down the edges. Scatter over the remaining marshmallows and drizzle the chocolate back and forth over the top to achieve a zig-zag effect. Crush the remaining biscuit, scatter the crumbs over the top of the semifreddo and serve immediately.

TIP
If the dulce de leche is quite thick when you spoon it onto the semifreddo it will sink. Heat gently in the microwave, and when it has cooled lightly drizzle it back and forth over the semifreddo to achieve a more even layer.

MISSISSIPPI
Mud Pie

A sticky chocolate pie that's great with vanilla ice cream, this is made using ingredients that are close to hand, and leftover biscuits are often used in the recipe for the base.

Serves 6–8

Prep: 30 mins, plus cooling   Cook: 35–40 mins

Ingredients

85 g/3 oz plain chocolate

85 g/3 oz unsalted butter

85 g/3 oz light muscovado sugar

2 eggs, beaten

100 ml/3½ fl oz single cream

1 tsp vanilla extract

Pastry

175 g/6 oz plain flour

25 g/1 oz cocoa powder

40 g/1½ oz light muscovado sugar

85 g/3 oz unsalted butter

2–3 tbsp cold water

10 g/¼ oz flour, for dusting

Topping

250 ml/9 fl oz whipping cream

85 g/3 oz plain chocolate

1. Preheat the oven to 200°C/400°F/Gas Mark 6. To make the pastry, sift the flour and cocoa powder into a bowl and stir in the sugar. Rub in the butter with your fingertips until the mixture resembles fine breadcrumbs. Add just enough water to bind to a dough.

2. Roll out the dough on a lightly floured work surface to a round large enough to line a 3-cm/1¼-inch deep, 20-cm/8-inch round tart tin. Use the pastry to line the tin. Prick the base with a fork, cover with a piece of greaseproof paper and fill with baking beans, then bake in the preheated oven for 10 minutes. Remove from the oven and take out the paper and beans. Reduce the oven temperature to 180°C/350°F/Gas Mark 4.

3. Put the chocolate and butter into a saucepan and heat over a low heat, stirring, until melted. Put the sugar and eggs into a bowl and whisk together until smooth, then stir in the chocolate mixture, cream and vanilla extract.

4. Pour the mixture into the pastry case and bake in the oven for 20–25 minutes or until just set. Leave to cool.

5. To make the topping, whip the cream until it just holds its shape, then spread over the pie. Put the chocolate into a bowl set over a saucepan of gently simmering water and heat until melted, then spoon into a piping bag and pipe decorations over the cream. Serve cold.

CHOCOLATE
fondue

Prepared in a slow cooker, this easy-to-make yet decadent dessert is a fun way to end a dinner party. Don't prepare the fruit until you're ready to serve the fondue.

Serves 4–6

Prep: 5 mins   Cook: 45–60 mins

Ingredients

10 g/¼ oz butter, for greasing

225 ml/8 fl oz double cream

350 g/12 oz plain chocolate, chopped into small pieces

1 tsp vanilla extract

To Serve

250 g/9 oz strawberries, hulled

2 bananas, peeled and sliced

1 apple, cut into chunks

marshmallows (optional)

1. Grease the inside of a slow cooker. Put the cream and chocolate into the slow cooker and stir to combine. Cover and cook on low, stirring occasionally, for 45–60 minutes, until the chocolate is completely melted. Stir in the vanilla extract.

2. Leave the mixture in the slow cooker or transfer to a fondue pot with a burner and serve immediately, with platters of strawberries, bananas, apple and marshmallows, if using, for dipping.

CHOCOLATE CHIP COOKIES
& Ice Cream Cake

Serves 8–10

This stunning layered cake will definitely impress and is well worth the effort of baking three separate bakes. It's delicious, too!

Prep: 30 mins, plus chilling and freezing   Cook: 15 mins

Ingredients

175 g/6 oz butter, softened

200 g/7 oz soft dark brown sugar

100 g/3½ oz caster sugar

1 egg, plus 1 egg yolk

1 tsp vanilla extract

250 g/9 oz plain flour

½ tsp salt

½ tsp bicarbonate of soda

325 g/11½ oz plain chocolate, broken into pieces

10 g/¼ oz butter, for greasing

2 litres/3½ pints vanilla ice cream

1. Using a food processor on high speed, cream together the butter, brown sugar and caster sugar for 8 minutes, or until pale and doubled in size. Reduce the speed of the food processor slightly and gradually add the egg, egg yolk and vanilla extract until well combined. Turn off the food processor and sift in the flour, salt and bicarbonate of soda. With the food processor on low, process the mixture until well combined, then add the chocolate and mix briefly. Chill in the refrigerator for 30 minutes.

2. Preheat the oven to 180°C/350°F/Gas Mark 4. Grease and line three 23-cm/9-inch round cake tins, at least one of which should be springform.

3. Remove the dough from the refrigerator and divide into three equal-sized pieces. Press the dough into the bases of the tins, making sure the thickness of the dough is even and that it goes right to the edges.

4. Cook in the preheated oven, in batches if necessary, for 15 minutes, or until just turning golden. Remove from the oven and leave to cool in the tins.

5. Meanwhile, remove the ice cream from the freezer to soften.

6. Remove two cookies from their tins. Keep the cookie in the springform tin as the cake base and build your cake with alternate, equal-sized layers of ice cream and cookie, finishing with the final – and best-looking – cookie on top. Push down gently to make sure the ice cream comes to the sides of the tin.

7. Place in the freezer for 4 hours. Remove from the freezer 10 minutes before serving and release and remove the springform. Cut into wedges and serve immediately.

TIP
The chocolate will set very quickly in the moulds, so make sure to sprinkle the sticks with the toppings as soon as possible after the sticks have been inserted.

CHOCOLATE CHUNK Sticks

Makes 10–15

Who would have thought that little blocks of chocolate on sticks would bring so much joy? Just dissolve them in hot milk for a perfect hot chocolate drink.

Prep: 5–10 mins, plus setting   Cook: 5–10 mins

Ingredients

200 g/7 oz plain chocolate, milk chocolate or white chocolate, or a mixture, finely chopped

2–4 tbsp of your choice of:

instant coffee granules

desiccated coconut

toasted nuts

mini marshmallows

chocolate vermicelli

edible glitter

1.2 litres/2 pints semi-skimmed milk or full-fat milk, to serve

1. Put the chocolate into a heatproof bowl set over a saucepan of gently simmering water and heat until melted. If you are using different chocolates melt them in separate bowls.

2. Divide the chocolate between silicone moulds, a silicone ice tray or small paper cases. Leave to cool slightly until the chocolate begins to thicken, then push a small wooden spoon, lollipop stick or wooden coffee stirrer into each mould so it stands upright.

3. While the chocolate is still soft, scatter each stick with your choice of toppings, then leave to set solid.

4. To serve, heat 1 mug of milk for each chocolate chunk stick. Remove any paper cases and stir a stick into each mug of milk until melted. Serve immediately.

Boozy Chocolate
Cheesecake

Serves 8

Cream liqueurs are the perfect ingredient in cheesecakes – they add a decadent yet smooth touch of alcohol to the nation's favourite dessert.

Prep: 30 mins, plus chilling   Cook: 10 mins

Ingredients

1 tbsp vegetable oil, for oiling

175 g/6 oz chocolate chip cookies

55 g/2 oz unsalted butter

crème fraîche and fresh fruit, to serve (optional)

Filling

225 g/8 oz plain chocolate, broken into pieces

225 g/8 oz milk chocolate, broken into pieces

55 g/2 oz golden caster sugar

350 g/12 oz cream cheese

425 ml/15 fl oz double cream, lightly whipped

3 tbsp Irish cream liqueur

1. Line the base of a 20-cm/8-inch round springform cake tin with baking paper and brush the sides with oil. Place the cookies in a polythene bag and crush with a rolling pin. Put the butter in a saucepan and gently heat until melted. Stir in the crushed cookies. Press into the base of the prepared tin and chill in the refrigerator for 1 hour.

2. Put the plain chocolate and milk chocolate into a heatproof bowl set over a saucepan of gently simmering water and heat until melted. Remove from the heat and leave to cool. Put the sugar and cream cheese into a bowl and beat together until smooth, then fold in the cream. Fold the melted chocolate into the cream cheese mixture, then stir in the liqueur.

3. Spoon the mixture into the tin and smooth the surface. Leave to chill in the refrigerator for 2 hours, or until quite firm. Transfer to a serving plate and cut into slices. Serve with crème fraîche and fresh fruit, if using.

TIP
You could serve this cheesecake with a glass of cream liqueur or even an Irish coffee as a treat on a cold day.

TOOLS

You don't really need high-tech equipment, but a few must-have items will make chocolate easier to handle, produce stunning decorations, and give your cakes and desserts that professional touch.

Chocolate equipment

Melting
Double boiler or bain-marie for melting chocolate on the hob over simmering water
Sugar thermometer or instant-read thermometer for checking the temperature of melting chocolate

Cooling
Marble slab for spreading and cooling chocolate

Decorating
Graters, coarse and fine
Swivel peeler for shaving curls
Cutters for hearts, flowers, stars, leaves

Piping cone (see box)
Piping nozzles
Brushes for painting leaves

Lifting
Palette knife for spreading chocolate and lifting fragile decorations
Skewers for transferring chocolate curls
Tweezers for lifting and arranging delicate decorations

Paper
Baking paper for piping decorations and spreading chocolate
Greaseproof paper for lifting and transferring chopped chocolate and for making piping cones (see opposite)

Baking equipment

Weighing and measuring
Measuring cups
Measuring jugs
Measuring spoons
Scales

Mixing
Bowls
Hand-held electric mixer
Stick blender
Food processor
Spatula
Wooden spoons

Pastry tools
Rolling pin
Silicone pastry mat
Marble slab
Pastry brush
Dough scraper

Trays and tins
Baking tray
Madeleine tin
Muffin tin
Cake tins
Swiss roll tin
Springform cake tins
Tart tins

Wrappers and cases
Baking paper
Greaseproof paper
Silicone sheets
Cupcake cases
Muffin cases

How to make a paper piping cone

- Cut out a square of greaseproof paper approximately 25 x 25 cm/ 10 x 10 inches. Fold in half diagonally to make two triangles (only one triangle is needed to make the bag).
- Hold the triangle by both corners of the longest side.
- Loop one corner inside the other to form a cone, with the tip of the cone facing away from you.
- Put one hand inside the cone, holding it together between your thumb and index finger.
- With your other hand, wrap the loose outside end around the cone to close up the point.
- Fold the top over to secure the cone.
- Snip off about 1 cm/½ inch from the tip of the cone, and drop in a piping nozzle. Otherwise snip off just a tiny bit from the tip and pipe directly from the bag.

Filling and closing the bag
- Stand the cone in a glass. Spoon the chocolate or icing into the bag, to no more than two-thirds full. It will be difficult to handle if you overfill. To close the bag, flatten the cone above the filling and fold over both corners to seal. Keep folding over the top as you pipe.

MOUSSE-AU-CHOCOLAT
Tartlets

Chocolate mousse is wonderfully creamy because plenty of air gets in when it is beaten. The flavour depends on the chocolate, so buy the best quality chocolate that you can.

Makes 6

Prep: 45 mins, plus chilling   Cook: 45 mins

Ingredients

Pastry

250 g/9 oz plain flour

pinch of salt

50 g/1¾ oz caster sugar

140 g/5 oz butter

1 egg

finely grated rind of 1 lemon

10 g/¼ oz flour, for dusting

Filling

375 ml/13 fl oz single cream

350 g/12 oz plain chocolate, 70% cocoa solids, broken into pieces

5 egg yolks

55 g/2 oz caster sugar

2½ tbsp water

sea salt flakes, to decorate (optional)

1. Preheat the oven to 180°C/350°F/Gas Mark 4. To make the pastry, put the flour, salt, sugar, butter, egg and lemon rind into a bowl and mix together. Roll the pastry into a ball, wrap in clingfilm and chill for 30 minutes in the refrigerator.

2. Roll out the pastry on a lightly floured work surface and ease it into six 10-cm/4-inch tartlet tins, then line them with baking paper and fill with baking beans. Bake in the preheated oven for 15 minutes, then remove the beans and paper and bake for a further 10 minutes.

3. To make the filling, heat the cream in a heatproof bowl set over a saucepan of gently simmering water, then add the chocolate and heat until melted. Remove from the heat and leave to cool to room temperature.

4. Put the egg yolks, sugar and water into a separate heatproof bowl set over a saucepan of simmering water and heat, whisking constantly, for 8–10 minutes until the mixture thickens. Remove from the heat, stir into the chocolate mixture and beat with a hand-held electric mixer for 5–6 minutes.

5. Pour the filling into the pastry cases. Carefully transfer to the refrigerator and chill for 2–3 hours, or until the filling is firm. Serve chilled, decorated with sea salt flakes, if using.

CHOCOLATE BAKED Alaska

Serves 6

This classic meringue and ice cream combo is a real showstopper! Use a good quality ice cream that won't melt too quickly and serve as soon as it comes out of the oven.

Prep: 30 mins, plus freezing   Cook: 5 mins

Ingredients

500 g/1 lb 2 oz luxury chocolate ice cream

6 ready-made chocolate brownies

2 large egg whites

115 g/4 oz caster sugar

10 g /¼ oz cocoa powder, for dusting

1. Line a 700-ml/1¼-pint pudding basin with clingfilm. Place the ice cream in the basin. Slice off any excess ice cream above the rim of the basin and cut this into smaller chunks. Push the chunks into the gaps around the main block of ice cream. Top with the chocolate brownies, cutting to fit, if necessary, and press down firmly. Place in the freezer for 15 minutes.

2. Preheat the oven to 220°C/425°F/Gas Mark 7. Put the egg whites into a clean, grease-free bowl and whisk until they hold firm peaks. Gradually whisk in the sugar, a spoonful at a time, to make a firm and glossy meringue.

3. Remove the basin from the freezer and turn out onto a baking sheet. Quickly spoon and spread the meringue all over the ice cream and the edge of the chocolate brownie base to cover completely. Bake in the preheated oven for 5 minutes, or until the meringue is just set and lightly browned. Serve immediately, lightly dusted with cocoa powder.

VARIATION

For individual versions, simply top each brownie with a scoop of the ice cream, then smother in the meringue. Reduce the cooking time to 3-4 minutes.

TIP

If you want perfect ice cream rounds, spoon the ice cream into a brownie tin to the thickness you desire. Use a cutter to cut out sharp-edged rounds of ice cream.

CHOCOLATE & TOASTED
Coconut Ice Cream Sandwiches

Makes 4

Take these incredible ice cream sandwiches further with a little fudge sauce. Remove the top cookies, add a spoon of sauce to the bottom cookies and replace the tops!

Prep: 30 minutes, plus cooling   Cook: 15 mins

Ingredients

50 g/1¾ oz unsalted butter

50 g/1¾ oz soft light brown sugar

½ tbsp golden syrup

50 g/1¾ oz self-raising flour

25 g/1 oz cocoa powder

25 g/1 oz chocolate chips

10 g/¼ oz flour, for dusting

6 tbsp desiccated coconut

4 scoops coconut ice cream

1. Preheat the oven to 180°C/350°F/Gas Mark 4. Line a baking sheet with baking paper. Beat together the butter and sugar until pale and fluffy. Add the golden syrup and beat again until combined. Fold in the flour, cocoa powder and chocolate chips.

2. Bring the dough together on a floured surface and divide into 8 equal portions. Shape each portion into a ball, then flatten the balls slightly with the palm of your hand and place on the prepared tray, spaced well apart to allow for spreading.

3. Transfer to the preheated oven and bake for 10–12 minutes until set. Leave to cool on the tray for 5 minutes, then transfer to a wire rack to cool completely.

4. Place the coconut in a heavy-based frying pan over a medium heat and cook, stirring, for 1–2 minutes until lightly golden. Remove from the heat and transfer to a plate to cool.

5. Place a scoop of ice cream on a cookie and, working quickly, spread it into a round. Sandwich closed with another cookie and gently roll through the toasted coconut. Repeat until you have used all the ice cream and cookies. Serve immediately.

CHOC BERRY
Rockets

Makes 8

Kids can have fun making these tasty iced treats by dipping them into chocolate and edible sprinkles to create their very own masterpieces.

Prep: 40 mins, plus cooling and freezing   Cook: 12–15 mins

Ingredients

400 g/14 oz raspberries

2 tbsp lemon juice

250 g/9 oz plain chocolate, roughly chopped

100 g/3½ oz hundreds and thousands

Sugar Syrup

90 g/3¼ oz caster sugar

200 ml/7 fl oz water

1. To make the sugar syrup, put the sugar and water into a small saucepan over a low heat and heat for 6–8 minutes until the sugar has dissolved. Increase the heat to high and bring to the boil, then reduce the heat to medium and simmer for 3–4 minutes. Remove from the heat and leave to cool.

2. Put the raspberries, lemon juice and sugar syrup in a blender and whizz until puréed. Press the purée through a fine metal sieve to remove the seeds. Pour into eight 100 ml/3½ fl oz ice pop moulds. Insert an ice pop stick into each mould and freeze for 3–4 hours, or until firm.

3. When the raspberry mixture is frozen, line a baking sheet with baking paper. To unmould the ice pops, dip the frozen moulds into warm water for a few seconds and gently release the pops while holding the sticks. Place them on the prepared baking sheet and return to the freezer for 1–2 hours.

4. When the ice pops are frozen, put the chocolate in a heatproof bowl set over a saucepan of gently simmering water and heat until melted. Remove from the heat and leave to cool slightly.

5. Tip the hundreds and thousands onto a sheet of baking paper. Dip each ice pop into the melted chocolate so it is covered to about half-way up, then roll it in the hundreds and thousands. Return to the prepared baking sheet and freeze for 10–20 minutes, or until ready to serve.

CHOCOLATE FUDGE
Ice Cream

Serves 4–6

Chocolate and fudge are a delicious combination, and become even more irresistible when combined with rich ice cream.

Prep: 20 mins, plus freezing   Cook: 25 mins

Ingredients

300 ml/10 fl oz milk

100 g/3½ oz plain chocolate, broken into pieces

25 g/1 oz butter

1 tsp vanilla extract

125 g/4½ oz caster sugar

75 g/2¾ oz golden syrup

4 eggs

300 ml/10 fl oz whipping cream

wafer sticks, to serve (optional)

1. Pour 175 ml/6 fl oz of the milk into a heavy-based saucepan. Add the chocolate, butter and vanilla extract and gently heat over a low heat, stirring constantly. Stir in the sugar and golden syrup and bring to the boil. Reduce the heat and simmer for 4 minutes, without stirring. Remove from the heat.

2. Put the eggs in a bowl and beat well. Add the chocolate mixture, stirring constantly.

3. Return the mixture to the rinsed-out pan and cook over a low heat for a further 10–15 minutes, stirring constantly, until the mixture is thick enough to coat the back of the wooden spoon. Do not allow the mixture to boil, or it will curdle.

4. Remove the mixture from the heat, add the remaining milk and the cream and stir together until smooth. Submerge the bottom of the pan in a bowl of ice-cold water, to stop the cooking process. Leave to cool for at least 1 hour, stirring from time to time to prevent a skin forming.

5. If using an ice cream maker, churn the mixture following the manufacturer's instructions. Alternatively, freeze in a freezer-proof container, uncovered, for 1–2 hours, or until it begins to set around the edges. Turn out into a bowl and stir with a fork until smooth. Return to the container and freeze for a further 2–3 hours, or until completely frozen.

6. To store, cover the container with a suitable lid. Remove the ice cream from the freezer and place in the refrigerator for 15–20 minutes before serving. Serve with wafer sticks, if using.

TRIPLE CHOCOLATE
Mousses

Makes
36

These smart-looking desserts can be prepared the day before you plan to serve them. You can even serve them frozen, and they are easier to slice if not fully thawed.

Makes
36

Prep: 45 mins, plus chilling and freezing   Cook: 2 mins

Ingredients

55 g/2 oz unsalted butter

1 tbsp cocoa powder

150 g/5½ oz digestive biscuits, crushed

milk chocolate curls, to decorate (optional)

Mousse

4 tbsp water

4 tsp powdered gelatine

115 g/4 oz plain chocolate, roughly chopped

115 g/4 oz milk chocolate, roughly chopped

115 g/4 oz white chocolate, roughly chopped

125 g/4½ oz unsalted butter

6 tbsp milk

6 eggs, separated

½ tsp vanilla extract

350 ml/12 fl oz double cream

1. Line a 20-cm/8-inch square deep, loose-based cake tin with two long strips of clingfilm, laid over each other in a cross, with an overhang on all sides of the tin. Melt the butter in a small saucepan, then stir in the cocoa powder and biscuit crumbs. Press the mixture into the tin in an even layer, then cover and chill in the refrigerator.

2. To make the mousse, put the water in a small heatproof bowl, then sprinkle the gelatine over the surface, making sure the powder is absorbed. Set aside for 5 minutes, then set the bowl over a saucepan of gently simmering water and heat for 5 minutes, stirring occasionally, until the gelatine is a clear liquid.

3. Put each type of chocolate in a separate heatproof bowl with one third of the butter and 2 tablespoons of milk. Place the bowls over saucepans of gently simmering water and heat until the chocolate has melted. Stir 2 egg yolks into each bowl, then remove from the heat. Stir 4 teaspoons of the gelatine into each bowl, then stir the vanilla extract into the white chocolate. Pour the cream into a fourth bowl and whisk until it holds soft peaks. Fold one third of the cream into each mixture. Whisk the egg whites in a large, clean bowl until they hold soft peaks, then divide them between the chocolate mixtures and fold in gently.

4. Pour the plain chocolate mousse into the tin and freeze for 15 minutes. Spoon over the white chocolate layer and freeze for 30 minutes. Gently whisk the milk chocolate layer to soften, then spoon it over and chill in the refrigerator overnight, or until set.

5. Lift the mousse out of the tin, pressing from the base. Peel off the clingfilm. Cut the mousse into 6 strips using a wet knife, then cut each strip into 6 small squares, wiping and wetting the knife frequently so that the layers don't become smeared. Arrange on small plates or saucers and decorate with chocolate curls, if using.

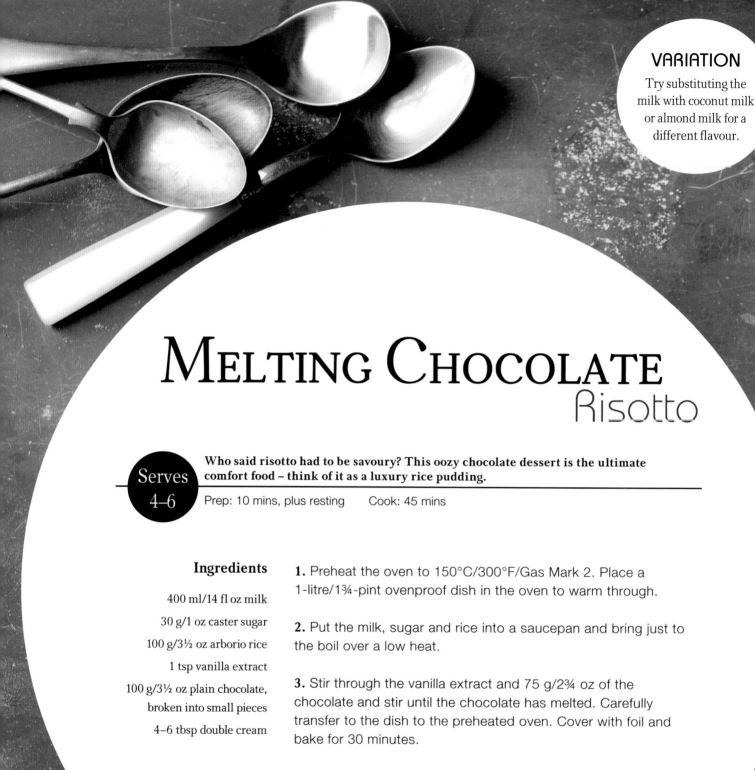

VARIATION

Try substituting the milk with coconut milk or almond milk for a different flavour.

MELTING CHOCOLATE
Risotto

Serves 4–6

Who said risotto had to be savoury? This oozy chocolate dessert is the ultimate comfort food – think of it as a luxury rice pudding.

Prep: 10 mins, plus resting   Cook: 45 mins

Ingredients

400 ml/14 fl oz milk

30 g/1 oz caster sugar

100 g/3½ oz arborio rice

1 tsp vanilla extract

100 g/3½ oz plain chocolate, broken into small pieces

4–6 tbsp double cream

1. Preheat the oven to 150°C/300°F/Gas Mark 2. Place a 1-litre/1¾-pint ovenproof dish in the oven to warm through.

2. Put the milk, sugar and rice into a saucepan and bring just to the boil over a low heat.

3. Stir through the vanilla extract and 75 g/2¾ oz of the chocolate and stir until the chocolate has melted. Carefully transfer to the dish to the preheated oven. Cover with foil and bake for 30 minutes.

4. Remove from the oven, stir well, re-cover and leave to rest for 5 minutes. Drizzle over the cream and swirl it into the risotto. Scatter with the remaining chocolate to serve.

MELTING CHOCOLATE
Sheet Cake

Serves 12–15

This luscious cake is light in texture and big on sweetness, and is a popular dessert at any small party or informal gathering.

Prep: 30 mins, plus cooling   Cook: 45 mins

Ingredients

10 g/¼ oz butter, for greasing

10 g/¼ oz flour, for dusting

250 g/9 oz plain flour

400 g/14 oz sugar

25 g/1 oz cocoa powder

1 tsp bicarbonate of soda

225 ml/8 fl oz water

115 g/4 oz butter

115 g/4 oz solid vegetable shortening

125 ml/4 fl oz buttermilk

2 eggs

1 tsp vanilla extract

Chocolate-pecan Frosting

115 g/4 oz butter

25 g/1 oz cocoa powder

90 ml/3 fl oz milk

450 g/1 lb icing sugar

1 tsp vanilla extract

120 g/4¼ oz pecan nuts, chopped and lightly toasted

1. Preheat the oven to 200°C/400°F/Gas Mark 6. Lightly grease a 33 x 23-cm/13 x 9-inch deep baking tin and dust with flour, shaking out any excess.

2. Combine the flour, sugar, cocoa powder and bicarbonate of soda in a large mixing bowl, stirring well to combine, then set aside until needed.

3. Combine the water, butter and shortening in a heavy saucepan and cook over a medium heat, stirring constantly with a wire whisk, until the butter is melted. Add the buttermilk, eggs and vanilla extract and whisk until combined. Pour the chocolate mixture over the flour mixture, stirring well.

4. Pour the batter into the prepared tin and bake in the preheated oven for 25—30 minutes, or until a cocktail stick inserted in the centre of the cake comes out clean. Leave to cool in the tin.

5. Meanwhile, make the frosting. Combine the butter, cocoa powder and milk in a medium-sized saucepan and cook over a low heat for 5 minutes, or until the butter is melted. Increase the heat to medium and bring to the boil, stirring constantly. Stir in the sugar, vanilla extract and pecan nuts and beat until smooth and the sugar is dissolved. Spread the frosting over the cooled cake.

TRIPLE CHOCOLATE
Ice Pops

Makes 8

For ultimate indulgence, these ice pops will surely hit all the right buttons with their creamy taste and triple chocolate hit. The pops can be frozen for up to 3 months.

Prep: 15 mins, plus cooling and freezing   Cook: 10 mins

Ingredients

300 ml/10 fl oz double cream

100 g/3½ oz plain chocolate, roughly chopped

100 g/3½ oz white chocolate, roughly chopped

100 g/3½ oz milk chocolate, roughly chopped

1. Divide the cream equally between three small saucepans. Put the plain chocolate in one of the pans, the white chocolate in another and the milk chocolate in the third.

2. Place each pan over a gentle heat and stir until the chocolate has melted and the mixture is smooth. Remove from the heat and leave to cool for 10–12 minutes.

3. Pour the dark chocolate mixture into eight 50 ml/1¾ fl oz ice pop moulds. Carefully pour the white chocolate mixture over the plain chocolate, then pour the milk chocolate mixture over the white chocolate. Insert the ice pop sticks and freeze for 3–4 hours, or until firm.

4. To unmould the ice pops, dip the frozen moulds in lukewarm water for a few seconds, then gently release the pops while holding the sticks.

TIP
To insert the ice pop sticks, cover the filled moulds with foil, make a small slit in the centre of the foil with a sharp knife, then insert the sticks.

SNAP

GOOEY CHOCOLATE
Chip Cookies

These little delights were invented accidentally in America in 1930 when some small pieces of chocolate accidentally fell into some plain cookie dough.

Makes 8

Prep: 10 mins   Cook: 10–12 mins

Ingredients

10 g/¼ oz unsalted butter, for greasing

175 g/6 oz plain flour, sifted

1 tsp baking powder

125 g/4½ oz unsalted butter, melted

85 g/3 oz light muscovado sugar

55 g/2 oz caster sugar

½ tsp vanilla extract

1 egg, beaten

125 g/4½ oz plain chocolate chips

1. Preheat the oven to 190°C/375°F/Gas Mark 5. Lightly grease two baking trays.

2. Place all of the ingredients in a large mixing bowl and beat until well combined.

3. Place tablespoons of the mixture on the prepared trays, spaced well apart to allow for spreading.

4. Bake in the preheated oven for 10–12 minutes, or until golden brown. Transfer to a wire rack and leave to cool.

Nutty Peppermint
Bark

Makes 25

Kids and adults alike will love this treat. If you can't get hold of peppermint candy canes, substitute them with any hard mint sweet.

Prep: 20 mins, plus setting   Cook: 3–4 mins

Ingredients

200 g/7 oz red-and-white striped peppermint candy canes, broken into pieces

500 g/1 lb 2 oz white chocolate, roughly chopped

50 g/1¾ oz pistachio nuts, chopped

50 g/1¾ oz walnuts, chopped

1. Line a 30 x 20-cm/12 x 8-inch baking tin with baking paper.

2. Put the broken candy canes into a large polythene bag and seal tightly. Using a rolling pin, bash the bag until the candy is crushed into small pieces.

3. Put the chocolate into a heatproof bowl set over a saucepan of gently simmering water and heat until melted. Remove from the heat and stir in three quarters of the candy.

4. Pour the mixture into the prepared tin, smooth the surface with a spatula and sprinkle over the chopped pistachio nuts and walnuts and the remaining candy. Press down very slightly to ensure they stick. Cover with clingfilm and chill in the refrigerator for 30 minutes, or until firm.

5. Break the bark into small, uneven pieces. Store in an airtight container in a cool, dry place for up to 2 weeks.

VARIATION

Use almond extract instead of vanilla extract to give the almond flavour a kick.

PLAIN CHOCOLATE &
Sea Salt Almond Biscotti

Makes 36

These twice-baked Italian crunchy biscuits are perfect for dunking in tea or serving after a meal with coffee.

Prep: 20 mins, plus cooling   Cook: 50 mins

Ingredients

450 g/1 lb plain flour

50 g/1¾ oz cocoa powder

1 tsp baking powder

1 tsp sea salt flakes

300 g/10½ oz caster sugar

150 g/5½ oz toasted flaked almonds

4 eggs, lightly beaten, plus 2 egg yolks

½ tbsp vanilla extract

10 g/¼ oz flour, for dusting

200 g/7 oz plain chocolate, broken into pieces

1. Preheat the oven to 180°C/350°F/Gas Mark 4. Line a baking sheet with greaseproof paper. Mix the flour, cocoa powder, baking powder, salt, sugar and flaked almonds together in a large bowl.

2. Stir in the eggs, egg yolks and vanilla extract. Mix well and bring together in a soft, smooth dough.

3. With floured hands shape the mixture into two 30-cm/12-inch logs, place the logs on two separate unlined baking sheets and bake in the preheated oven for 30 minutes until set on top. Leave to cool for 10 minutes. Reduce the oven temperature to 150°C/300°F/Gas Mark 2.

4. Use a serrated knife to cut each log diagonally into 1-cm/½-inch thick slices. Lay the slices on the baking sheets and bake for a further 20 minutes, turning them over after 10 minutes. Transfer to a wire rack and leave to cool completely.

5. Meanwhile, put the chocolate into a heatproof bowl set over a saucepan of gently simmering water and heat until melted.

6. Dip the cooled biscotti into the melted chocolate, then transfer them to the prepared baking sheet and leave to set. Store in an airtight container.

DOUBLE CHOCOLATE & Cherry Cookies

Makes 30

The sour cherries cut through the richness of the chocolate in these tasty little cookies, but don't be fooled – they are extremely indulgent and calorific.

Prep: 15 mins, plus cooling   Cook: 12–15 mins

Ingredients

225 g/8 oz unsalted butter, softened

140 g/5 oz caster sugar

1 egg yolk, lightly beaten

2 tsp vanilla extract

250 g/9 oz plain flour

25 g/1 oz cocoa powder

pinch of salt

350 g/12 oz plain chocolate, chopped

55 g/2 oz dried sour cherries

1. Preheat the oven to 190°C/375°F/Gas Mark 5. Line two baking sheets with baking paper.

2. Put the butter and sugar into a bowl and mix well with a wooden spoon, then beat in the egg yolk and vanilla extract. Sift the flour, cocoa powder and salt into the mixture, add the chocolate and sour cherries and stir until thoroughly combined.

3. Scoop up tablespoons of the mixture and shape into balls. Put them on the prepared baking sheets, spaced well apart, and flatten slightly.

4. Bake in the preheated oven for 12–15 minutes. Leave to cool on the baking sheets for a few minutes, then transfer to wire racks to cool completely.

TIP
Use a plain chocolate with a high percentage of cocoa solids for this recipe.

CHOCOLATE-DIPPED
Pumpkin Seed Brittle

Makes 10–12

Classic peanut brittle is given a makeover with crunchy pumpkin seeds, a little plain chocolate and a sprinkling of sea salt.

Prep: 10 mins, plus setting   Cook: 30 mins

Ingredients

10 g/¼ oz butter, for greasing

300 g/10½ oz sugar

55 g/2 oz golden syrup

100 ml/3½ fl oz cold water

40 g/1½ oz butter

¼ tsp bicarbonate of soda

85 g/3 oz pumpkin seeds, warmed

50 g/1¾ oz plain chocolate, broken into pieces

¼ tsp sea salt flakes

1. Lightly grease a large, heavy-duty baking sheet. Line a board with baking paper. Put the sugar, golden syrup and water into a large, heavy-based saucepan and heat gently, stirring with a wooden spoon, until the sugar has dissolved. Stir in the butter and heat until melted.

2. Bring the mixture to the boil, without stirring, then cover and boil for 2–3 minutes. Uncover and clip a sugar thermometer to the side of the pan. Continue to boil the mixture steadily, without stirring, until it reaches 154°C/310°F (the 'hard crack' stage) on the thermometer – this will take about 25 minutes.

3. Remove the pan from the heat and stir in the bicarbonate of soda and pumpkin seeds (take care, as the mixture may bubble up). Slowly pour the mixture onto the prepared baking sheet, spreading it out to a 30-cm/12-inch square with a palette knife.

4. Leave to stand for a few minutes until the brittle is beginning to set, then mark out about 10 thin strips with a greased long-bladed knife. Leave to stand in a cool place until completely cold and set.

5. Put the chocolate into a small heatproof bowl set over a saucepan of gently simmering water and heat until melted. Remove from the heat and stir until smooth, then leave to cool for 10 minutes.

6. Using a sharp knife, cut the brittle into long thin strips (some strips may break into shorter pieces). Dip one end of each piece of brittle in the melted chocolate. Place on the prepared board and sprinkle the chocolate with a few sea salt flakes. Leave to stand in a cool place until set.

TIP
Don't boil the mixture too rapidly or it may burn and stick to the base of the saucepan.

CHILLI & CARDAMOM
Chocolate Thins

Makes 40

These simple treats are perfect for kids to make. They're also ideal for putting into a pretty box and giving as a present.

Prep: 30 mins, plus setting   Cook: 5–10 mins

Ingredients

Chilli Plain Chocolate Thins

200 g/7 oz plain chocolate, roughly chopped

large pinch of hot chilli powder

edible glitter, to decorate (optional)

Cardamom White Chocolate Thins

200 g/7 oz white chocolate, roughly chopped

½ tsp cardamom seeds, crushed

25 g/1 oz pistachio nuts, finely chopped

chopped pistachio nuts and edible glitter, to decorate (optional)

1. Line four baking trays with foil petit four cases.

2. For the chilli plain chocolate thins, put the plain chocolate in a heatproof bowl set over a saucepan of gently simmering water and heat until melted. Remove from the heat and stir in the chilli powder.

3. Drop teaspoons of the chocolate mixture into half of the petit four cases. Scatter over a little edible glitter before the chocolate sets, if using. Leave to set in a cool place, but not in the refrigerator, for 1–2 hours.

4. For the cardamom white chocolate thins, put the white chocolate in a heatproof bowl set over a saucepan of gently simmering water and heat until melted. Remove from the heat and stir in the cardamom and the pistachio nuts.

5. Drop teaspoons of the white chocolate mixture into the remaining petit four cases. Scatter over some chopped pistachio nuts and a little edible glitter, if using, before the chocolate sets. Leave to set in a cool place, but not in the refrigerator, for 1–2 hours. Store in an airtight container in a cool, dry place for up to 5 days.

TIP
If you don't have petit four cases, drop teaspoons of the mixture onto baking trays lined with non-stick baking paper.

VARIATION

Invent your own combo with your favourite nuts, dried fruit or even sweets! Or try swapping the chocolate crispies for flavoured ones, such as coffee, mint or orange.

BANOFFEE CHOCOLATE Slab

Makes 1

Make a unique gift for friends by preparing a delicious chocolate slab. It just seems a shame to break something so beautiful!

Prep: 15 mins, plus setting   Cook: 10 mins

Ingredients

200 g/7 oz milk chocolate, finely chopped

200 g/7 oz plain chocolate, finely chopped

200 g/7 oz white chocolate, finely chopped

40 g/1½ oz dried banana chips

50 g/1¾ oz fudge pieces

1 tbsp chocolate crispies

1. Line a 22 x 26-cm/8½ x 10½-inch baking tray with greaseproof paper. Place the milk chocolate, plain chocolate and white chocolate in separate heatproof bowls set over saucepans of gently simmering water and heat until melted. Leave to cool for 1–2 minutes.

2. Working quickly, pour the milk chocolate into the left side of the prepared tray, then pour the white chocolate into the right side of the tray. Pour the plain chocolate into the centre.

3. Using a knife, carefully drag the different chocolates into each other to create a swirled effect. Scatter over the banana chips, fudge pieces and chocolate crispies. Leave to set in a cool place for approximately 3 hours until set hard. Do not chill.

WHITE CHOCOLATE &
Macadamia Nut Cookies

Makes 16

These chunky chocolate and nut cookies are so quick and easy to make, they'll soon become a family favourite!

Prep: 25 mins   Cook: 12–14 mins

Ingredients

10 g/¼ oz butter, for greasing

115 g/4 oz butter, softened

115 g/4 oz soft light brown sugar

1 tbsp golden syrup

175 g/6 oz self-raising flour

55 g/2 oz macadamia nuts, roughly chopped

55 g/2 oz white chocolate, chopped into chunks

1. Preheat the oven to 180°C/350°F/Gas Mark 4. Grease two large baking sheets.

2. Put the butter and sugar into a bowl and beat together until pale and creamy, then beat in the golden syrup. Sift in the flour, add the nuts and mix to a rough dough.

3. Divide the dough into 16 even-sized pieces, shape each piece into a ball and place the balls on the prepared baking sheet, spaced well apart to allow for spreading. Slightly flatten each ball with your fingertips and top with the chocolate chunks, lightly pressing them into the dough.

4. Bake in the preheated oven for 12–14 minutes, or until the cookies are just set and pale golden. Leave them to cool on the baking sheets for 5 minutes, then transfer to a wire rack to cool completely.

TIP
If the cookies have spread during baking, reshape them with a knife when they come out of the oven.

DARK CHOCOLATE BAR
with Dried Cherries & Hazelnuts

Makes 16

Rich dark chocolate, dried fruit and crunchy hazelnuts make this bar a really special treat for a tea break or for morning coffee.

Prep: 15 mins, plus chilling   Cook: 10 mins

Ingredients

70 g/2½ oz dried cherries

55 g/2 oz hazelnuts, chopped

350 g/12 oz plain chocolate, chopped

15 g/½ oz crispy rice cereal

1. Line a 28 x 23-cm/11 x 9-inch baking tin with baking paper. Combine the cherries and hazelnuts in a small bowl and mix well.

2. Put the chocolate in a heatproof bowl set over a saucepan of gently simmering water and heat until melted. Remove from the heat and stir in the rice cereal.

3. Pour the chocolate mixture into the prepared tin and smooth it into a thin layer with a rubber palette knife. Immediately top with the cherries and nuts, sprinkling them evenly over the top and pressing them into the chocolate with the palm of your hand. Chill in the refrigerator for at least 1 hour until completely set.

4. Break into pieces and serve at room temperature.

CHOCOLATE FUDGE BROWNIE
Quinoa Cookies

Makes 26

Quinoa flour is made by grinding quinoa seeds and is a great grain- and gluten-free alternative to wheat flours.

Prep: 30 mins, plus cooling   Cook: 12–14 mins

Ingredients

55 ml/2¼ fl oz coconut oil

100 g/3½ oz plain chocolate, 70% cocoa solids, broken into pieces

55 g/2 oz quinoa flour

1 tbsp cocoa powder

1 tsp bicarbonate of soda

½ tsp ground cinnamon

2 eggs

150 g/5½ oz light muscovado sugar

1 tsp vanilla extract

1. Preheat the oven to 190°C/375°F/Gas Mark 5. Line three baking sheets with non-stick baking paper.

2. Place the oil and chocolate in a bowl set over a saucepan of gently simmering water and heat for 5 minutes, or until the chocolate has melted, then stir to mix.

3. Put the flour, cocoa powder, bicarbonate of soda and cinnamon into a separate bowl and stir together.

4. Put the eggs, sugar and vanilla extract into a large mixing bowl and whisk together until thick and frothy. Gently fold in the oil and chocolate mixture, then add the flour mixture and stir until smooth.

5. Drop dessertspoons of the mixture on the prepared trays, spaced well apart, then bake in the preheated oven for 7–9 minutes, until crusty and cracked, and still slightly soft to the touch. Leave to cool and harden slightly on the trays, then lift off the paper and pack into an airtight tin. Eat within 3 days.

WHITE CHOCOLATE &
Lemon Squares

Makes 9

Tangy lemon squares drenched in creamy white chocolate make the perfect teatime treat.

Prep: 20 mins, plus cooling and setting   Cook: 45–50 mins

Ingredients

10 g/¼ oz butter, for greasing

100 g/3½ oz unsalted butter

190 g/6½ oz caster sugar

120 g/4¼ oz plain flour, plus 2 tbsp

pinch of salt

½ tsp vanilla extract

3 eggs

1 tbsp lemon zest

100 ml/3½ fl oz lemon juice

100 g/3½ oz white chocolate

25 g/1 oz plain chocolate

9 fresh raspberries

1. Preheat the oven to 180°C/350°F/Gas Mark 4. Grease a 20-cm/8-inch square baking tin and line with baking paper.

2. Place the butter, 50 g/1¾ oz of the sugar, the flour and salt in a food processor and pulse until fine and grainy. Add the vanilla extract and pulse until the mixture comes together.

3. Turn out into the prepared tin and press down evenly with the back of a spoon. Transfer to the preheated oven and bake for 16–18 minutes until lightly browned.

4. Meanwhile, whisk together the eggs, the remaining sugar, the lemon zest, lemon juice and the remaining 2 tablespoons of flour until smooth and combined. Pour over the base and return to the oven for 30 minutes until the filling is set. Leave to cool in the tin.

5. Put the white chocolate into a heatproof bowl set over a saucepan of gently simmering water and heat until melted. Leave to cool slightly before pouring over the cake. Leave to set.

6. Put the plain chocolate into a separate heatproof bowl set over a saucepan of gently simmering water and heat until melted. Drizzle over the cake. Leave to set, then cut the cake into squares, place a raspberry on top of each square and serve.

MINI CRANBERRY &
Ginger Florentines

Makes 48

These crisp, chewy bites are an Italian classic and make a marvellous present at Christmas – or any time of the year!

Prep: 30 mins, plus cooling and setting   Cook: 15–20 mins

Ingredients

10 g/¼ oz butter, for greasing

10 g/¼ oz flour, for dusting

70 g/2½ oz muscovado sugar

55 g/2 oz clear honey

100 g/3½ oz unsalted butter

50 g/1¾ oz desiccated coconut

70 g/2½ oz flaked almonds

1 tbsp finely chopped mixed peel

1 tbsp finely chopped crystallized ginger

100 g/3½ oz dried cranberries

50 g/1¾ oz plain flour

250 g/9 oz plain chocolate, roughly chopped

1. Preheat the oven to 180°C/350°F/Gas Mark 4. Lightly grease four 12-hole mini muffin tins (the base of each hole should be 2 cm/¾ inch in diameter), then lightly dust with flour.

2. Put the sugar, honey and butter into a heavy-based saucepan. Heat gently, stirring, until the sugar has dissolved, tilting the pan to mix the ingredients together. Stir in the coconut, almonds, mixed peel, crystallized ginger, cranberries and flour.

3. Put small teaspoons of the mixture into the prepared tins. Bake in the preheated oven for 10–12 minutes, or until golden brown. Leave to cool in the tins for 1 hour. Using a palette knife, transfer to a wire rack to firm up.

4. Meanwhile, put the chocolate into a heatproof bowl set over a saucepan of gently simmering water and heat until melted.

5. Dip each florentine into the melted chocolate so the base is covered. Place on a wire rack, chocolate side up, and leave to set for 1 hour. Store in an airtight container in a cool, dry place for up to 2 days.

SNAP

Master the techniques of chocolate decoration and you'll be able to transform an ordinary cake or dessert into something really special.

Piping

If you have a steady hand, pipe directly onto the surface. If it's your first time, trace your chosen pattern onto a piece of paper. Place the pattern under a sheet of non-stick baking paper and tape it securely in place.

If using a nozzle, insert it in the piping cone, otherwise pipe from the tip. Half-fill the cone with melted chocolate and fold over the top.

Using gentle pressure, pipe onto the paper, following the tracing. Point the cone upwards when you finish to prevent any chocolate leaking out.

Leave to chill, then carefully move into place with a palette knife.

Tempering chocolate

Tempering chocolate stabilizes the crystals, making it glossy and easier to mould when making decorations. The simplest method is to melt the chocolate in a bowl set over gently simmering water, then put the bowl in a larger bowl of cold water and stir to cool. Reheat as follows:

Plain chocolate: Melt to 40–45°C/104–113°F, cool to 27–28°C/80–82°F, reheat to 31–32°C/89–90°F.

Milk chocolate: Melt to 32.5°C/90°F, cool to 27–28°C/80–82°F, reheat to 30°C/86°F.

White chocolate: Melt to 30.5°C/87°F, cool to 27°C/80°F, reheat to 28°C/82°F.

Caraque and cones

Pour melted chocolate onto a marble slab or chilled baking sheet, spreading evenly with a palette knife. For caraque, hold a long knife at a 45° angle, and push the knife away from you, scraping into the chocolate. For cones, position the knife tip securely and scrape in a circle.

Curls and shavings

Curls are made from room-temperature chocolate; shavings from chilled chocolate. Using a swivel peeler, shave the sides of the chocolate. Depending on the temperature, curls or shavings will fall from the block. Avoid touching them with your fingers – use a palette knife to move them.

Leaves

Use pesticide-free non-poisonous leaves with short stems – stiff shiny ones such as citrus or rose are best. Wash and pat dry thoroughly. Paint a thick layer of melted chocolate onto the veined side. Place the coated leaves on a baking tray lined with non-stick baking paper. Leave to stand in a cool room until completely set.

Holding the stem, carefully pull the leaf away from the chocolate. Use a small palette knife or tweezers to arrange on a cake.

CHOCOLATE & OAT
Cookies

Makes 15

All the goodness of oats, combined with all the luscious sweetness of chocolate hazelnut spread and the crunchiness of hazelnuts in one delicious little morsel.

Prep: 5 mins, plus cooling   Cook: 15 mins

Ingredients

10 g/¼ oz butter, for greasing

85 g/3 oz unsalted butter

175 g/6 oz chocolate hazelnut spread

175 g/6 oz porridge oats

70 g/2½ oz blanched hazelnuts, chopped

1. Preheat the oven to 200°C/400°F/Gas Mark 6. Grease a baking sheet.

2. Place the butter and chocolate hazelnut spread in a saucepan and heat gently until just melted.

3. Add the oats and hazelnuts to the chocolate mixture and stir to combine thoroughly.

4. Shape the mixture into 15 equal-sized balls, then press onto the prepared baking sheet. Bake in the preheated oven for 10–12 minutes. Remove from the oven and leave until firm, then transfer to a wire rack to cool completely.

Peanut Butter
S'mores

Serves 1–2

These delicious little mouthfuls are traditional campfire treats, but are far too luscious to keep for those rare summer nights around the fire.

Prep: 5 mins, plus cooling   Cook: 5 mins

Ingredients

115 g/4 oz smooth peanut butter

6 graham crackers

85 g/3 oz plain chocolate, broken into squares

1. Preheat the grill to high. Spread the peanut butter on one side of each cracker.

2. Place the chocolate pieces on four of the crackers and invert the remaining crackers on top.

3. Toast the s'mores under the preheated grill for about 1 minute until the filling starts to melt. Turn carefully using tongs. Leave to cool slightly, then serve.

VARIATION

If you can't get graham crackers, digestive biscuits will work just as well.

TIP
Don't touch the caramel! It's hot! And do not walk away as it will suddenly brown and burn.

White Chocolate,
Sour Cherry & Pistachio Brittle

Makes 8–10

You don't need a sugar thermometer to make brittle, just a little time and patience. And smashing it up is a lot of fun!

Prep: 10 mins, plus cooling and setting   Cook: 10–15 mins

Ingredients

1 tbsp vegetable oil, for oiling

100 g/3½ oz pistachio nuts, roughly chopped

200 g/7 oz golden caster sugar

100 g/3½ oz unsalted butter

pinch of salt

120 ml/3¾ fl oz water

300 g/10½ oz white chocolate, chopped

50 g/1¾ oz dried sour cherries, chopped

1. Oil a baking sheet or baking tray. Scatter over half the nuts and set aside.

2. Place the sugar, butter, salt and water in a small saucepan and gently heat until the sugar dissolves. Bring to the boil and cook, stirring occasionally, for approximately 5 minutes until light golden brown.

3. Carefully tip the caramel over the nuts and leave to cool for 20 minutes until set.

4. Put the chocolate into a heatproof bowl set over a saucepan of gently simmering water and heat until melted. Remove from the heat, pour it over the brittle and tilt to cover.

5. Scatter over the remaining nuts and the cherries. Leave to set in a cool place but not in the refrigerator. Break into shards and store in an airtight container.

GRASSHOPPER MINT
Chocolate Bark

Makes 18–20

This mint-flavoured chocolate bark is very simple to make but looks amazing and tastes wonderful too! Break it into shards and serve as an after-dinner treat.

Prep: 20 mins, plus cooling and chilling   Cook: 20 mins

Ingredients

vegetable oil, for oiling

350 g/12 oz plain chocolate, broken into pieces

300 g/10½ oz white chocolate, broken into pieces

1½ tsp peppermint extract

1 tsp green liquid food colouring

1. Lightly oil a 33 x 23-cm/13 x 9-inch Swiss roll tin and line the base and sides with baking paper.

2. Put the plain chocolate into a heatproof bowl set over a saucepan of gently simmering water and heat until melted. Remove from the heat and stir until smooth. Set aside 4 tablespoons of the melted chocolate in a small, heatproof bowl.

3. Pour the remaining melted chocolate into the prepared tin and gently level the surface with a palette knife. Firmly tap the tin on a work surface to remove any air bubbles. Leave to stand for 15 minutes, or until the tin is cool, then chill in the refrigerator for 30–40 minutes, or until firmly set.

4. Put the white chocolate into a separate heatproof bowl set over a saucepan of gently simmering water and heat until melted. Remove from the heat, leave to cool for 5–10 minutes, then beat in the peppermint extract and food colouring. The chocolate will start to thicken, but continue beating for 1–2 minutes until it has a smooth and spreadable consistency.

5. Spoon the mint-flavoured chocolate over the set chocolate and spread quickly with a palette knife (don't worry if the plain chocolate underneath melts slightly). If necessary, re-melt the reserved plain chocolate by placing the bowl over a saucepan of gently simmering water. Drizzle it over the mint chocolate layer and lightly drag a fork through to create a swirled effect.

6. Chill in the refrigerator for a further 40–50 minutes, or until the bark is firmly set. Remove from the tin, peel off the paper and break into chunks to serve.

TIP
For an extra minty flavour, roughly crush 2–3 mint humbugs and scatter over the top of the bark before it sets.

STRAWBERRY & WHITE
Chocolate Napoleons

**Makes
8**

These beautiful fancies may look light and airy, but appearances can be deceptive – they
are both rich and delicious and will make any occasion special.

Prep: 40 mins, plus cooling and chilling   Cook: 6–8 mins

Ingredients

6 sheets frozen filo pastry,
thawed

4–6 sprays cooking oil spray

1½ tsp caster sugar

500 g/1 lb 2 oz fresh
strawberries, hulled
and sliced

2 tbsp icing sugar, to decorate

Filling

100 g/3½ oz white chocolate,
chopped

5 tbsp plus 125 ml/4 fl oz
water

125 g/4½ oz caster sugar

3 egg whites

¼ tsp cream of tartar

1. Preheat the oven to 180°C/350°F/Gas Mark 4 and line a large
baking tray with baking paper. Carefully separate one filo sheet
from the others, lay it on a work surface, and spray it all over with
the cooking spray. Sprinkle with about ¼ teaspoon of the sugar.
Lay another sheet of filo on top and repeat the steps until you
have three layers. Cut the stack of filo sheets into 12 squares
and transfer to the prepared tray. Repeat with the remaining three
sheets of filo pastry so that you have 24 squares. Bake in the
preheated oven for 6–8 minutes until lightly coloured. Leave to
cool completely on the tray.

2. To make the filling, put the white chocolate and the 5
tablespoons of water in a heatproof bowl set over a saucepan
of gently simmering water and heat, stirring frequently, until the
chocolate has melted and the mixture is smooth. Set aside.

3. In a small saucepan, combine the sugar with the remaining
water and bring to the boil. Cook, stirring, for about 5 minutes or
until the mixture begins to thicken.

4. Whisk the egg whites in a large bowl until foamy. Add the
cream of tartar and beat for a further 3 minutes, gradually
increasing the speed, until they hold soft peaks. Slowly beat in the
warm sugar mixture, then beat on high until the mixture holds stiff,
glossy peaks. Whisk one third of the egg white mixture into the
melted chocolate until well combined. Whisk in the remaining egg
white mixture. Transfer the mixture to a bowl, cover and chill in the
refrigerator for at least 1 hour.

5. Just before serving, lay eight filo squares on the work surface.
Top each with about 2 tablespoons of the white chocolate
mousse, then top this with four to five strawberry slices and
another square of filo. Repeat with another layer of mousse and
strawberries. Finish with a filo square and a dusting of icing sugar.
Serve immediately.

MOLTEN-CENTRED
Chocolate Cupcakes

Makes 8

These luxurious cupcakes, with their gooey melted chocolate centres, are the ultimate in sweet indulgence. For the best results, use a really good quality chocolate.

Prep: 20 mins, plus cooling   Cook: 20 mins

Ingredients

85 g/3 oz self-raising flour

1 tbsp cocoa powder

55 g/2 oz butter, softened

55 g/2 oz caster sugar

1 large egg

55 g/2 oz plain chocolate

10 g/¼ oz icing sugar, for dusting

1. Preheat the oven to 190°C/375°F/Gas Mark 5. Put eight paper cases in a bun tin.

2. Sift the flour and cocoa powder into a large bowl. Add the butter, caster sugar and egg and beat with a hand-held electric mixer until smooth.

3. Spoon half of the mixture into the paper cases. Using a teaspoon, make an indentation in the centre of each. Break the chocolate into 8 squares and place a piece in each indentation, then spoon the remaining cake mixture on top.

4. Bake in the preheated oven for 20 minutes, or until risen and firm to the touch. Leave the cupcakes in the tin for 2–3 minutes, then serve warm, dusted with the icing sugar.

CHOCOLATE & HAZELNUT
Marshmallows

Makes 25

These elegant little treats combine creamy chocolate hazelnut spread, crunchy toasted hazelnuts and dreamy marshmallow.

Prep: 45 mins, plus cooling and setting   Cook: 25 mins

Ingredients

1 tbsp sunflower oil, for oiling

1 tbsp cornflour

1 tbsp icing sugar

25 large marshmallows

3 tbsp chocolate hazelnut spread, warmed

25 blanched hazelnuts, toasted

100 g/3½ oz plain chocolate, broken into pieces, to decorate

1. Lightly oil a 20-cm/8-inch shallow square cake tin. Line the base and two sides with baking paper, then lightly oil the paper.

2. Sift the cornflour and icing sugar into a bowl. Use this mixture to dust the lined tin, tapping it firmly so the mixture coats the base and sides completely.

3. Put the marshmallows into a large saucepan with a little water and heat over a medium heat, stirring constantly, for 8–10 minutes, or until melted. Gently fold in the warmed chocolate hazelnut spread.

4. Pour the mixture into the prepared tin and gently level the surface. Lightly dust the top with some of the coating mixture, then arrange the hazelnuts evenly on top of the marshmallow. Leave to set, uncovered, in a cool, dry place for 4–5 hours.

5. Run the tip of a lightly oiled knife along the unlined sides of the tin to release the marshmallow. Using the lining paper, gently lift out the marshmallow and place on a chopping board. Cut into 25 squares, wiping and re-greasing the knife frequently. Dust the marshmallows with the coating mixture.

6. To decorate, put the chocolate into a heatproof bowl set over a saucepan of gently simmering water and heat until melted. Remove from the heat and stir until smooth. Leave to cool for 10 minutes. Spoon the chocolate into a paper piping bag and snip off the end. Pipe lines of chocolate over the marshmallows. Leave in a cool place to set. Store in an airtight container for up to 5 days.

TIP

For a luxurious treat,
serve the meringues
with whipped
cream.

CHOCOLATE & ORANGE
Swirl Meringues

These are the kind of huge meringues you gaze at through a patisserie window. They are very easy to make – you'll be the envy of all your friends!

Makes 8

Prep: 20 mins, plus cooling   Cook: 1 hour 15 mins

Ingredients

100 ml/3½ fl oz blood orange juice

25 g/1 oz caster sugar

1½ tbsp triple sec

2–4 drops of red food colouring

80 g/2¾ oz plain chocolate, broken into small pieces

Meringues

6 egg whites

350 g/12 oz caster sugar

2 tsp cornflour

2 tsp white wine vinegar

1. Preheat the oven to 120°C/250°F/Gas Mark ½. Line a large baking sheet with baking paper or a silicone sheet. Place the orange juice, sugar, triple sec and food colouring in a small saucepan and bring to the boil over a medium heat. Boil for 10 minutes until thick and syrupy. Set aside to cool slightly.

2. Put the chocolate into a heatproof bowl set over a saucepan of gently simmering water and heat until melted. Leave to cool for 10 minutes.

3. To make the meringues, put the egg whites into a large bowl and whisk until they hold soft peaks. Add the sugar, a tablespoon at a time, whisking after each addition. Add the cornflour and vinegar and continue to whisk until the meringue is thick and glossy and holds stiff peaks.

4. Drizzle half the chocolate over the meringue, then drizzle over half the syrup. Spoon half the egg mixture onto the prepared baking sheet in 4 large dollops.

5. Drizzle the remaining chocolate and syrup over the remaining meringue mixture in the bowl and spoon out 4 more large meringues onto the baking sheet. Transfer to the preheated oven and bake for 1 hour. Turn off the oven, open the oven door slightly and leave the meringues to cool in the oven.

DARK CHOCOLATE
Roulade

Serves 6–8

A roulade is always an impressive dessert. The contrasting white and dark chocolate and bright red raspberry drizzle makes this one a work of art.

Prep: 45 mins   Cook: 15–20 mins

Ingredients

10 g/¼ oz butter, for greasing

175 g/6 oz plain chocolate, broken into squares

4 large eggs, separated

115 g/4 oz caster sugar

10 g/¼ oz cocoa powder, sifted, for dusting

225 g/8 oz white chocolate, broken into squares

225 g/8 oz mascarpone cheese

10 g/¼ oz icing sugar, for sprinkling

Raspberry Coulis

300 g/10½ oz raspberries

2 tbsp icing sugar

1. Preheat the oven to 180°C/350°F/Gas Mark 4. Grease a 33 x 23-cm/13 x 9-inch Swiss roll tin and line with greaseproof paper.

2. Put the plain chocolate in a heatproof bowl set over a saucepan of gently simmering water and heat until melted. Remove from the heat and leave to cool slightly.

3. Put the egg yolks and sugar into a bowl and whisk until pale and thick. Whisk the egg whites in a separate grease-free bowl until they hold soft peaks. Quickly stir the melted chocolate into the egg yolk mixture, then fold in the whisked egg whites. Spread the mixture in the prepared tin and bake in the preheated oven for 15–20 minutes, until risen and firm. Dust a sheet of greaseproof paper with the cocoa powder. Turn out the roulade onto the paper, cover with a clean tea towel and leave to cool.

4. Meanwhile, put the white chocolate in a heatproof bowl set over a saucepan of gently simmering water and heat until melted. Remove from the heat and leave to cool slightly. Stir into the mascarpone cheese, mixing until it has a spreadable consistency.

5. Uncover the roulade, remove the greaseproof paper and spread with the white chocolate cream. Use the paper to roll up the roulade to enclose the filling (do not worry if it cracks).

6. To make the raspberry coulis, put the raspberries and sugar into a food processor and process to a smooth purée. Press through a sieve to remove the seeds.

7. Sprinkle the roulade with icing sugar and serve in slices with the raspberry coulis poured over.

CHOCOLATE
Samosas

These folded triangles can be filled with a variety of ingredients, typically cooked leftovers, and then deep fried. Here, they've been turned into a delightful dessert.

Makes 16

Prep: 1 hour, plus chilling   Cook: 10–15 mins

Ingredients

250 ml/9 fl oz whipping cream

250 g/9 oz plain chocolate chips

250 g/9 oz plain flour

100 ml/3½ fl oz ghee

oil, for deep-frying

1. Put the cream into a small saucepan and bring to the boil over a medium heat. Put the chocolate chips into a bowl, pour over the boiling cream and stir until melted. Chill in the refrigerator for 1 hour.

2. Meanwhile, sift the flour into a mixing bowl, add the ghee and rub in. If the dough is too stiff, gradually add a little cold water. Keep covered with a damp cloth.

3. Divide the dough into 16 equal-sized pieces and roll out each piece into a long rectangle. Put 1 teaspoon of the filling onto one end of the rectangle and fold over the dough repeatedly to make a triangle shape.

4. Heat enough oil for deep-frying in a large saucepan to 180–190°C/350–375°F, or until a cube of bread browns in 30 seconds. Add the samosas, in batches if necessary, and cook over a medium heat until crisp and golden. Do not overcrowd the pan, and take care that the oil is brought back to the correct temperature in between each batch. Drain on kitchen paper and leave to cool for 5 minutes. Serve warm.

CHOCOLATE & CHERRY
Sorbet

Serves 4

The chocolate makes this sorbet rich and thick, while the frozen cherries add instant glamour.

Prep: 10 mins, plus freezing and softening   Cook: 10 mins

Ingredients

300 ml/10 fl oz cold water

3 tbsp stevia (sugar substitute)

25 g/1 oz cocoa powder

¼ tsp ground allspice

4 cherries, stoned and chopped, plus 4 whole cherries to decorate

70 g/2½ oz plain chocolate, 85% cocoa solids, broken into small pieces

1. Pour the water into a saucepan, then add the stevia, cocoa powder, allspice and chopped cherries. Lightly whisk together, then slowly bring to the boil over a medium-high heat.

2. Remove from the heat and leave to cool for 2–3 minutes. Stir in the chocolate. Pour the mixture into a freezerproof container, cover with a lid and freeze for 4 hours, or until set. Stir with a fork every 30 minutes to break up the ice crystals. Put the whole cherries in the freezer.

3. Take the sorbet out of the freezer 10 minutes before you serve to allow it to soften. Scoop it into glasses or small bowls, decorate each with a frozen cherry and serve immediately.

VARIATION
Frozen raspberries would make a good alternative to the cherries in this sorbet. Add them with the chocolate in Step 3.

TIP
Save old jars or bottles
and fill with the fudge to
make delicious home-
made gifts.

HOME-MADE CHOCOLATE
Fudge Sauce

**Makes
600 ml/
1 pint**

**This simple sauce is your new best friend. Keep a jar in the fridge to pair with
ice cream, to use in baking, on pancakes or just to eat decadently off a spoon!**

Prep: 10 minutes, plus cooling   Cook: 10 mins

Ingredients

175 ml/6 fl oz double cream

175 g/6 oz golden syrup

75 g/2¾ oz soft dark brown
sugar

40 g/1½ oz cocoa powder

¼ tsp salt

175 g/6 oz plain chocolate

2 tbsp butter

1 tsp vanilla extract

1. Place the cream, golden syrup, sugar, cocoa powder, salt and
half the chocolate in a medium-sized saucepan. Heat over a low-
medium heat, stirring occasionally, until melted and combined.

2. Increase the heat and bring just to the boil, then reduce to a
low simmer and cook for 3 minutes, stirring occasionally.

3. Remove from the heat and stir in the remaining chocolate with
the butter and vanilla extract. Stir until smooth and leave to cool
slightly before transferring to jars or bottles.

4. The sauce will thicken while it cools, so before serving reheat
it in the microwave on Low for a few seconds, or in a saucepan
over a low heat for 30 seconds–1 minute until still thick but
pourable. Store in the refrigerator and use within 2 weeks.

CHOCOLATE MERINGUE Kisses

These elegant little 'kisses' of melt-in-the-mouth meringue dipped in chocolate make a very good canapé or gift.

Makes 40

Prep: 40 mins, plus cooling and setting   Cook: 50 mins

Ingredients

3 egg whites

1 tsp raspberry vinegar

150 g/5½ oz caster sugar

1 tsp cornflour

2 tbsp cocoa powder, sifted

200 g/7 oz plain chocolate, roughly chopped

1. Preheat the oven to 160°C/325°F/Gas Mark 3. Line three baking trays with non-stick baking paper.

2. Whisk the egg whites in a large, clean mixing bowl until they hold stiff, moist-looking peaks. Gradually whisk in the vinegar and sugar, a tablespoon at a time, until thick and glossy. Using a large metal spoon, gently fold in the cornflour and cocoa.

3. Spoon the mixture into a piping bag fitted with a large star nozzle and pipe forty 2.5-cm/1-inch 'kisses' onto the prepared baking trays.

4. Put the trays in the preheated oven, then immediately reduce the oven temperature to 120°C/250°F/Gas Mark ½. Bake for 45 minutes, or until crisp on the outside. Transfer the meringues to a wire rack, still on the paper, and leave to cool for 1 hour, then peel off the paper.

5. Meanwhile, put the chocolate in heatproof bowl set over a saucepan of gently simmering water and heat until melted.

6. Line the baking trays with more baking paper. Dip the bases of the meringue kisses in the melted chocolate and place them, chocolate side up, on the prepared baking trays. Leave to set for 1 hour. Store in an airtight container in a cool, dry place for up to 2 weeks.

COMBINE

Whether you're making cakes, desserts, confectionery or drinks, combining chocolate with well-matched ingredients makes it an even more memorable treat.

Popular combinations

Chocolate and spices

Spices and chocolate are a natural culinary match, as the Aztecs knew when they flavoured their famous chocolate drink, xocolatl, with chilli and cinnamon.

Chocolate and chillies work well – the rich creaminess of the chocolate tempers the heat of the chilli. Good-quality black pepper is another successful match. The heat stands up to the richness of chocolate, but it's subtler than chilli heat.

Sweet spices such as cinnamon, cardamom and nutmeg have always been used in baking. Combined with chocolate they are even more delicious and aromatic.

Salt

Used in the correct proportion, salt balances sweet flavours. It is also an essential flavour enhancer – just a pinch will round out a cake or dessert. Salt also provides texture – crunchy sea salt combined with plain chocolate is simply exquisite.

Flowers

Fragrant flowers such as rose and lavender combine well with plain chocolate. The most widely used pairing, however, is vanilla – the fermented seed pods of the orchid. Vanilla shows up in one form or another in most chocolate bars today.

Fruit

Chocolate and fruit is a match made in heaven – in cakes and desserts, as well as chocolates themselves. Dried fruits such as sultanas and raisins are a classic combination, but tangy and flavoursome fresh fruits tickle the taste buds too.

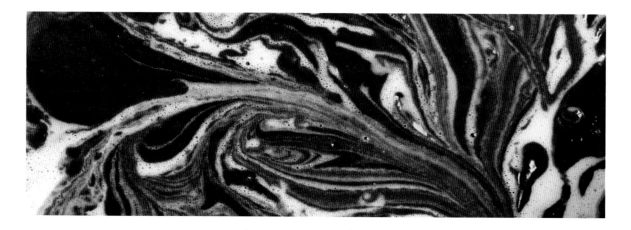

Flavour pairings table

Check out the table for more details of what goes with what, and when to use it.

Ingredient		Plain Chocolate	Milk Chocolate	White Chocolate	Use
Spices	Cardamom	★ ★	★	–	Cakes, desserts, confectionery
	Chilli	★ ★	★	–	Desserts, drinks, confectionery
	Cinnamon	★	★	★	Cakes, desserts, drinks, confectionery
	Ginger	★ ★	★	–	Cakes, desserts, drinks, confectionery
	Nutmeg	★	★	★	Cakes, desserts, drinks
	Pepper	★ ★	★	★	Cakes, desserts, confectionery
Salt	Sea Salt	★ ★	★	–	Cakes, desserts, confectionery
Flowers	Lavender	★	★	–	Desserts, confectionery
	Rose	★	★	–	Desserts, confectionery
	Vanilla	★ ★	★ ★	★ ★	Cakes, desserts, drinks, confectionery
Fruit	Apricots	★	★	★	Cakes, desserts, confectionery
	Bananas	★ ★	★ ★	★	Cakes, desserts, confectionery
	Cherries	★ ★	★ ★	★	Cakes, desserts, confectionery
	Lemons	★ ★	★	★ ★	Cakes, desserts, confectionery
	Limes	★ ★	–	★	Cakes, desserts, confectionery
	Oranges	★ ★	★ ★	★	Cakes, desserts, confectionery
	Pears	★ ★	★ ★	–	Cakes, desserts, confectionery
	Raisins	★	★	–	Cakes, desserts, confectionery
	Raspberries	★ ★	★ ★	★	Cakes, desserts, confectionery
	Strawberries	★	★	★	Cakes, desserts, confectionery
Herbs	Mint	★ ★	★	–	Desserts, confectionery
	Rosemary	★ ★	–	–	Desserts, confectionery
	Thyme	★	–	–	Confectionery
Nuts	Almonds	★	★	★	Cakes, desserts, confectionery
	Chestnuts	★	★	–	Cakes, desserts
	Coconut	★ ★	★ ★	★	Cakes, desserts, confectionery
	Hazelnuts	★	★	–	Cakes, desserts, confectionery
Vegetable	Beetroot	★	★	–	Cakes, desserts

* well paired; * * very well paired; – not reccomended

BIG CHOCOLATEY
Banana Split

Makes 1

Bananas seem to have been designed to be combined with chocolate, and this old-fashioned sweet treat is still a big favourite.

Prep: 5 mins   Cook: None

Ingredients

1 large banana

500 ml/18 fl oz chocolate ice cream

250 ml/9 fl oz clotted cream

100 ml/3½ fl oz dulce de leche (caramel sauce)

55 g/2 oz pecan nuts, crushed

55 g/2 oz maraschino cherries

1. Peel and split the banana lengthways then place on a rectangular serving plate.

2. Put 3 large scoops of chocolate ice cream on top, then scoop the clotted cream on top.

3. Drizzle over the dulce de leche, top with the crushed nuts and cherries and serve immediately.

TIP
Add scoops of vanilla ice cream and up the quantity of dulce de leche for a side-splitting banana-buster!

CHOCOLATE FONDANTS
with Toffee Sauce

This restaurant favourite is surprisingly easy to make and can be prepared in advance. The toffee sauce makes them an extra special indulgent treat.

Makes 10

Prep: 25 mins, plus chilling   Cook: 17–20 mins

Ingredients

150 g/5½ oz unsalted butter

4 tsp cocoa powder

150 g/5½ oz plain chocolate, roughly chopped

2 eggs, plus 2 egg yolks

125 g/4½ oz caster sugar

25 g/1 oz plain flour

10 g/¼ oz icing sugar, sifted, for dusting

Toffee Sauce

55 g/2 oz unsalted butter

55 g/2 oz light muscovado sugar

1 tbsp clear honey

150 ml/5 fl oz double cream

1. Melt 25 g/1 oz of the butter in a small saucepan, then brush it over the insides of ten 125-ml/4-fl oz ovenproof ramekins. Sift a little cocoa into each ramekin, then tilt to coat evenly, tapping out any excess.

2. Put the chocolate and the remaining butter in a heatproof bowl set over a saucepan of gently simmering water and heat, stirring occasionally, until melted.

3. Put the eggs, egg yolks and caster sugar into a mixing bowl and whisk together until thick and frothy and the whisk leaves a trail when raised above the mixture. Sift in the flour, then gently fold it in.

4. Fold the melted chocolate mixture into the egg mixture until smooth. Pour it into the prepared ramekins, cover and chill in the refrigerator for 1 hour, or overnight if time allows.

5. To make the toffee sauce, put the butter, sugar and honey into a heavy-based saucepan and heat gently for 3–4 minutes, or until the butter has melted and the sugar dissolved, then boil for 1–2 minutes, stirring, until it begins to smell of toffee and thicken. Remove from the heat and stir in the cream.

6. Preheat the oven to 180°C/350°F/Gas Mark 4. Take the ramekins out of the refrigerator and leave to stand at room temperature for 10 minutes. Bake in the preheated oven for 10–12 minutes, or until well risen, the tops are crusty and the centres still slightly soft. Reheat the sauce over a low heat, if needed.

7. Dust the desserts with sifted icing sugar. Serve immediately with the sauce in a jug for pouring.

BROWN BUTTER & CHOCOLATE
Fudge Croissant Sandwiches

Makes 6

These are not your average croissants and make a wonderful weekend breakfast treat with a cup of steaming cappuccino.

Prep: 10 mins   Cook: 10 mins

Ingredients

50 g/1¾ oz caster sugar

20 g/¾ oz cornflour

1 egg

½ tsp vanilla extract

200 ml/7 fl oz milk

6 ready-made croissants

6 tbsp ready-made fudge sauce

2 tbsp unsalted butter

pinch of salt

1. Whisk together the sugar, cornflour, egg and vanilla extract in a bowl.

2. Pour the milk into a small saucepan and bring just to the boil. Remove from the heat and pour it into the egg mixture, whisking constantly until combined.

3. Transfer to a clean saucepan, place over a low heat and heat, whisking constantly, until smooth and thick. Transfer to a bowl and cover the surface with clingfilm to prevent a skin forming. Leave to cool for 30 minutes.

4. Cut the croissants in half and spread a tablespoon of fudge sauce over the bottom half of each. Spoon the custard mixture over the fudge, then top with the remaining croissant halves.

5. Melt the butter in a large frying pan over a low-medium heat and add the salt. Cook for 1 minute, or until lightly browned. Add the croissants to the pan and cook for 1–1½ minutes on each side until lightly crisped. Gently transfer the croissants to plates and serve immediately.

VARIATION
Try adding slices of
banana or strawberry
between the layers.

CHOCOLATE
Filo Parcels

Makes 18

Filo pastry is a popular staple in eastern Mediterranean kitchens. It is very similar to central European flaky pastry, but the leaves are thinner and more translucent.

Prep: 15–20 mins, plus cooling   Cook: 10 mins

Ingredients

10 g/¼ oz butter, for greasing

85 g/3 oz ground hazelnuts

1 tbsp finely chopped fresh mint

125 ml/4 fl oz soured cream

2 eating apples, peeled and grated

55 g/2 oz plain chocolate, melted

9 sheets filo pastry, about 15 cm/6 inches square

55–85 g/2–3 oz butter, melted

10 g/¼ oz icing sugar, sifted, for dusting

1. Preheat the oven to 190°C/375°F/Gas Mark 5. Grease a baking tray. Mix the nuts, mint and soured cream in a bowl. Add the apples, stir in the chocolate and mix well.

2. Cut each pastry sheet into 4 squares. Brush a square with butter, then place a second square on top and brush with butter.

3. Place 1 tablespoon of the chocolate mixture in the centre of a square, then bring up the corners and twist together. Repeat until all of the pastry and filling have been used.

4. Place the parcels on the prepared tray and bake in the preheated oven for about 10 minutes, until crisp and golden. Remove from the oven and leave to cool slightly.

5. Dust with icing sugar and serve.

GOOEY CHOCOLATE
Pudding

Serves 4–6

This chocolatey variation on a very traditional everyday dessert will have everyone clamouring for second helpings!

Prep: 5 mins, plus chilling   Cook: 25 mins

Ingredients

100 g/3½ oz sugar

4 tbsp cocoa powder

2 tbsp cornflour

pinch of salt

350 ml/12 fl oz milk

1 egg, beaten

55 g/2 oz butter

½ tsp vanilla extract

double cream, to serve (optional)

1. Put the sugar, cocoa powder, cornflour and salt into a heatproof bowl, stir and set aside.

2. Pour the milk into a saucepan and heat over a medium heat until just simmering. Do not bring to the boil.

3. Keeping the pan over a medium heat, spoon a little of the simmering milk into the sugar mixture and blend, then stir this mixture into the milk in the pan. Beat in the egg and half the butter and reduce the heat to low.

4. Simmer for 5–8 minutes, stirring frequently, until the mixture thickens. Remove from the heat and add the vanilla extract and the remaining butter, stirring until the butter is melted and has been absorbed.

5. Serve hot or chilled, with cream for pouring over, if using. If chilling the pudding, spoon it into a serving bowl and leave to cool completely, then press clingfilm onto the surface to prevent a skin forming and chill in the refrigerator until required.

White Chocolate &
Peppermint Marshmallows

Makes 24

The traditional peppermint and chocolate combo is presented here in frothy, prettily decorated individual marshmallows that are just right for a party.

Prep: 45 mins, plus cooling and setting   Cook: 25 mins

Ingredients

1 tbsp sunflower oil, for oiling

1 tbsp cornflour

1 tbsp icing sugar

25 large marshmallows

2–4 drops peppermint extract

100 g/3½ oz white chocolate, broken into pieces

4 small candy canes, roughly crushed

1. Lightly oil two 12-hole silicone cupcake tins and place them on two baking sheets. Sift together the cornflour and icing sugar into a bowl. Use a little of this mixture to lightly dust each hole.

2. Put the marshmallows into a large saucepan with a little water and heat over a medium heat, stirring constantly, for 8–10 minutes, or until melted. Stir in the peppermint extract.

3. Meanwhile, put the chocolate into a heatproof bowl set over a saucepan of gently simmering water and heat until melted. Remove from the heat and stir until smooth. Leave to cool for 10 minutes, stirring occasionally.

4. Gently fold three quarters of the melted chocolate into the marshmallow mixture. Spoon the mixture into the prepared tins.

5. Spoon a small swirl of the remaining melted chocolate onto each marshmallow and sprinkle with the crushed candy canes. Lightly dust the tops with a little of the coating mixture. Leave to set, uncovered, in a cool, dry place for 3–4 hours.

6. Carefully remove the marshmallows from the trays. Lightly dust the bases and sides with the remaining coating mixture. Store in an airtight container for up to 5 days.

SALTED CARAMEL
Lava Cakes

Serves 4

Since salted caramel first graced our tables its crown has never been shifted.
These little lava cakes are a happy duo of sophistication and homeliness.

Prep: 20 mins   Cook: 15 mins

Ingredients

10 g/¼ oz butter, for greasing

240 g/8¾ oz plain chocolate, chopped into rough chunks

100 g/3½ oz butter

2 eggs, plus 2 egg yolks

110 g/3¾ oz caster sugar

35 g/1¼ oz plain flour

1 tsp sea salt flakes

4 tbsp dulce de leche (caramel sauce)

10 g/¼ oz cocoa powder, for dusting

1. Preheat the oven to 200°C/400°F/Gas Mark 6. Grease four 200-ml/7-fl oz dariole moulds. Place 200 g/7 oz of the chocolate in a small saucepan with the butter and heat over a low heat until smooth and combined.

2. Place the eggs, egg yolks and sugar in a large bowl and beat together until well combined. Pour over the melted chocolate mixture, stir to combine, then fold in the flour.

3. Half fill each of the prepared moulds with the chocolate mixture. Mix the salt into the dulce de leche and place 1 tablespoon of the mixture in the centre of each mould. Top each with a piece of the remaining chocolate. Fill the moulds with the remaining chocolate mixture to 5 mm/¼ inch from the tops of the moulds.

4. Place on a baking tray and bake in the preheated oven for 16 minutes. The cakes should spring back when pressed gently. Carefully turn out the cakes and dust with the cocoa powder. Serve immediately.

VARIATION

Swap the dulce de leche for peanut butter or chocolate spread.

REAL HOT
Chocolate

Serves 1–2

This is the perfect winter warmer. Once you've tried it, you'll probably become addicted. Top with whipped cream for a really indulgent treat.

Prep: 5 mins   Cook: 45 mins

Ingredients

40 g/1½ oz plain chocolate, broken into pieces

300 ml/10 fl oz milk

chocolate curls, to decorate (optional)

1. Place the chocolate in a large, heatproof jug. Place the milk in a heavy-based saucepan and bring to the boil. Pour about one quarter of the milk onto the chocolate and leave to stand until the chocolate is soft.

2. Whisk the milk and chocolate mixture until smooth. Return the remaining milk to the heat and bring back to the boil, then pour onto the chocolate, whisking constantly.

3. Pour into mugs or large cups and decorate with chocolate curls, if using.

FROZEN HOT CHOCOLATE
with Hazelnut Liqueur

Serves 4

Just when you thought the weather was getting too warm for hot chocolate, here is a luxurious chilled version, laced with delicious hazelnut liqueur.

Prep: 5 mins, plus cooling   Cook: 20 mins

Ingredients

85 g/3 oz plain chocolate, chopped

2 tbsp caster sugar

1 tbsp cocoa powder

350 ml/12 fl oz skimmed milk

900 g/2 lb ice cubes

1 banana

4 tbsp hazelnut liqueur

1. Put the chocolate into a heatproof bowl set over a saucepan of gently simmering water and heat until melted.

2. Add the sugar and cocoa powder and heat, stirring constantly, until the sugar is completely dissolved. Remove from the heat and slowly add the milk, stirring until combined. Leave to cool to room temperature.

3. Transfer the chocolate mixture to a blender and add the ice, banana and hazelnut liqueur. Blend until well combined and frothy. Pour into four glasses and serve immediately.